AQA GCSE
Physics
The Workbook

This book is for anyone doing **AQA GCSE Physics**.

It's full of **tricky questions**... each one designed to make you **sweat**
— because that's the only way you'll get any **better**.

There are questions to see **what facts** you know. There are questions
to see how well you can **apply those facts**. And there are questions
to see what you know about **how science works**.

It's also got some daft bits in to try and make the whole
experience at least vaguely entertaining for you.

What CGP is all about

Our sole aim here at CGP is to produce the highest
quality books — carefully written, immaculately presented
and dangerously close to being funny.

Then we work our socks off to get them
out to you — at the cheapest possible prices.

Contents

PHYSICS 2(ii) — ELECTRICITY AND THE ATOM

PHYSICS 3(i) — FORCES AND WAVES

PHYSICS 3(ii) — MAGNETISM AND STARS

Published by Coordination Group Publications Ltd.

Editors:
Ellen Bowness, Sarah Hilton, Sharon Keeley, Ali Palin, Alan Rix, Ami Snelling, Julie Wakeling.

Contributors:
Tony Alldridge, Peter Cecil, Steve Coggins, Vikki Cunningham, Andrew Furze, Giles Greenway, Frederick Langridge, Barbara Mascetti, Steve Parkinson, Andy Williams.

ISBN-10: 1 84146 465 1
ISBN-13: 978 1 84146 465 7

With thanks to Ian Francis, Steve Parkinson and Glenn Rogers for the proofreading.

Groovy website: www.cgpbooks.co.uk

Printed by Elanders Hindson Ltd, Newcastle upon Tyne.
Jolly bits of clipart from CorelDRAW®

Heat Transfer

Q1 a) Indicate whether each of the following statements is true or false.

True False

   i) Heat radiation is sometimes called infrared radiation. ☐ ☐

   ii) Conduction involves the transfer of energy between moving particles. ☐ ☐

   iii) Hot objects do not absorb radiation. ☐ ☐

   iv) Convection always involves a moving liquid or gas. ☐ ☐

   v) Cold objects do not emit radiation. ☐ ☐

b) Write out corrected versions of the **false** statements.

....

....

....

Q2 Three flasks, each containing 100 ml of water, are placed in closed boxes. The water in the flasks and the air in the boxes are at different temperatures, as shown.

A   Air in box 55°C   Water 60°C

B   Air in box 50°C   Water 65°C

C   Air in box 65°C   Water 70°C

Which flask will cool fastest?
Give a reason for your answer.

Flask .... will cool fastest because ....

....

Q3 Each sentence below contains two mistakes. Write out a correct version of each.

a) Infrared radiation is emitted from the centre of hot solid objects, but not from liquids or gases.

....

b) The fins on a motorcycle engine decrease the amount of radiation emitted and keep the engine warm.

....

....

Heat Transfer

Q4   Three pupils are talking about how we get heat energy from the Sun.

 Peter:
The Sun warms the Earth by convection.

 Lucy:
The Sun warms us because it is much hotter than the Earth.

 Edmund:
If the Sun were bigger, it would give us more heat.

For each pupil, circle whether they are right or wrong, and explain your answer.

a)   Peter is right / wrong because

....

b)   Lucy is right / wrong because

....

c)   Edmund is right / wrong because

....

Q5   Simon fills a shiny container with boiling water and measures its temperature every 5 minutes. The graph shows his results.

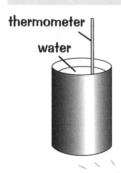
thermometer
water

Why does the drop in temperature get less and less each time?

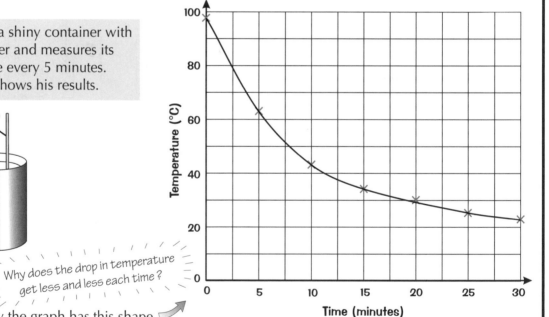

a)   Explain why the graph has this shape.

....

....

b)   Simon's friend Jason repeats the experiment. He uses the same volume of boiling water in a can which is shallower and wider but otherwise identical.

Sketch on the graph above the results you would expect **Jason** to get.

Top Tips: Hot tea in a cold mug, surrounded by cold air, loses more heat to the mug (and air) than it absorbs from it. The greater the temperature difference, the faster your tea cools down.

Physics 1a — Energy and Electricity

Heat Radiation

Q1 Give a scientific reason why steel **electric kettles** are often made very **shiny**.

....

....

Q2 Tick the correct boxes below to show whether the sentences are true or false.

                                                              True False

a) The amount of heat radiation absorbed by a surface depends only on its colour.

b) The hotter a surface is, the more heat it radiates.

c) Good absorbers of heat are also good emitters of heat.

d) Thermos flasks can keep hot things hot but cannot keep cold things cold.

e) Silver survival blankets help the body to absorb heat.

Q3 Ms Smith and Mr Jones each put a **solar hot water panel** on the roof of their houses.

Ms Smith's house

Mr Jones' house

Write down two reasons why Ms Smith gets more hot water than Mr Jones.

....

....

Q4 Complete the following sentences by circling the correct words.

a) Dark, matt surfaces are **good** / **poor** absorbers and **good** / **poor** emitters of heat radiation.

b) The best surfaces for radiating heat are **good** / **poor** absorbers and **good** / **poor** emitters.

c) The best materials for making survival blankets are **good** / **poor** absorbers and **good** / **poor** emitters.

d) The best surfaces for solar hot water panels are **good** / **poor** absorbers and **good** / **poor** emitters.

Heat Radiation

Q5 Tim did an investigation using a **Leslie's cube**.
Each surface on the cube had a different combination of **colour** and **texture**.

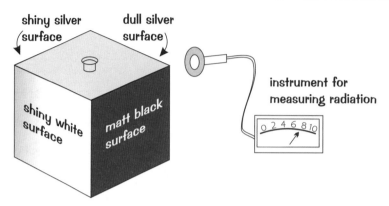

shiny silver surface   dull silver surface

shiny white surface   matt black surface

instrument for measuring radiation

Tim measured the heat radiation coming from each surface. His results are shown below.

Surface	Reading	Colour and Texture
A	10	
B	4	dull silver
C	4	
D	2	

a) Complete the table to show which was:

i) the **matt black** surface.

ii) the **shiny silver** surface.

iii) the **shiny white** surface.

b) Tim's friend Julie copied his results for the experiment.
She then wrote a conclusion —

    "Dull silver and shiny white surfaces always emit the same amount of radiation."

Explain what is wrong with Julie's conclusion.

....

....

c) Which of the surfaces A to D would be best to use for the outside of a refrigerator?
Explain your answer.

....

....

Heat Conduction

Q1 Tick to show whether the sentences are true or false.

		True	False
a)	Conduction involves **energy** passing between **vibrating particles**.	☐	☐
b)	Some **metals** are very **poor** conductors.	☐	☐
c)	**Solids** are usually better **conductors** of heat than liquids and gases.	☐	☐
d)	**Plastic** is a **poor** conductor because it contains **free electrons**.	☐	☐

Q2 George picks up a piece of wood and a metal spoon. Both have the same temperature: 20 °C.

Explain why the metal spoon feels **colder** to the touch than the piece of wood.

....

....

Q3 In summer, Jamie wears a cotton vest.
In winter he wears a string vest.
He always wears the same kind of shirt.

Jamie's summer vest

Jamie's winter vest

Jamie finds that a string vest keeps him warmer than a cotton vest. Why is this?

....

....

Q4 Sajid, Mamphela and Ruth are discussing why copper is a good conductor of heat.

Sajid says, **"Copper is a great conductor because it's got electrons in it."**

Mamphela says, **"It conducts well because it's shiny."**

Ruth says, **"It conducts well because all its particles have kinetic energy."**

Each pupil has made at least one mistake. Explain one mistake made by:

a) Sajid ....

....

b) Mamphela ....

....

c) Ruth ....

....

Heat Convection

Q1 a) Tick the sentences to show whether they are true or false.

True False

i) In a hot water tank, an immersion heater is usually placed at the bottom of the tank. ☐ ☐

ii) The hotter the water, the denser it is. ☐ ☐

iii) Convection currents happen when hot water displaces cold water. ☐ ☐

iv) Convection currents can happen in water but not in air. ☐ ☐

b) Write a correction for each false sentence.

....

....

....

Q2 Tim tested a convector heater in three rooms.
The rooms all had the **same volume**, but they were **different shapes**.

Tall room

Cubic room

Long room

In which room would you expect the heater to work best? Explain your answer.

....

....

Q3 Match each observation with an explanation.

The very bottom of a hot water tank stays cold... | because water doesn't conduct much heat.

Warm air rises... | because heat flows from warm places to cooler ones.

A small heater can send heat all over a room... | because it is not so dense.

Heat Convection

Q4   Convection can make water flow round the pipes in a house, without using a pump.
Miss Jenkins demonstrates this to her pupils using the apparatus below.

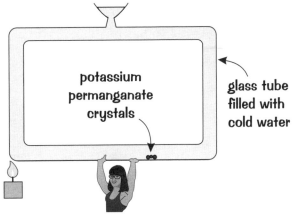

a)   Draw arrows on the diagram to show which way the water moves.

b)   Explain what happens to the water above the heat to cause the convection current.

....

....

....

....

....

Q5   Sam uses the apparatus shown to investigate heat transfer in water.

He heats the middle of the tube with a Bunsen flame.
The ice at the top of the tube melts quickly,
but the ice at the bottom does not melt.

What does this experiment show about conduction and
convection in water? Explain your answer.

Ice floating
at the top

Glass tube full
of cold water

Ice weighted
so it stays at
the bottom

....

....

....

....

___

Top Tips: Remember, **convection** only happens in **fluids** (liquids and gases), **conduction**
happens fastest in **solids**, but **all** objects emit and absorb heat **radiation**.

Physics 1a — Energy and Electricity

Useful Heat Transfers

Q1   List four features of a **Thermos flask** that reduce non-useful heat transfers.
State whether each reduces conduction, convection or radiation.

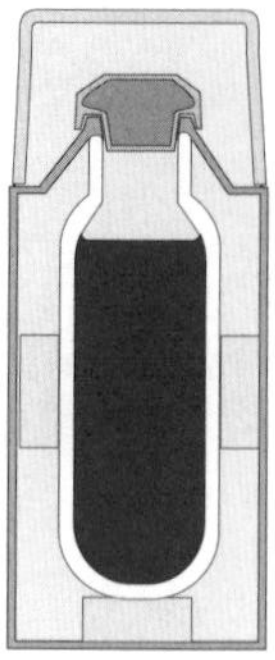

1. ....

2. ....

3. ....

4. ....

Q2   Natasha did an experiment to test how well plastic foam keeps a beaker of water hot.

She put different thicknesses of foam around three beakers.
The water in each beaker started off at 100 °C.

After 10 minutes Natasha read the temperatures. Her results are shown on the diagram below.

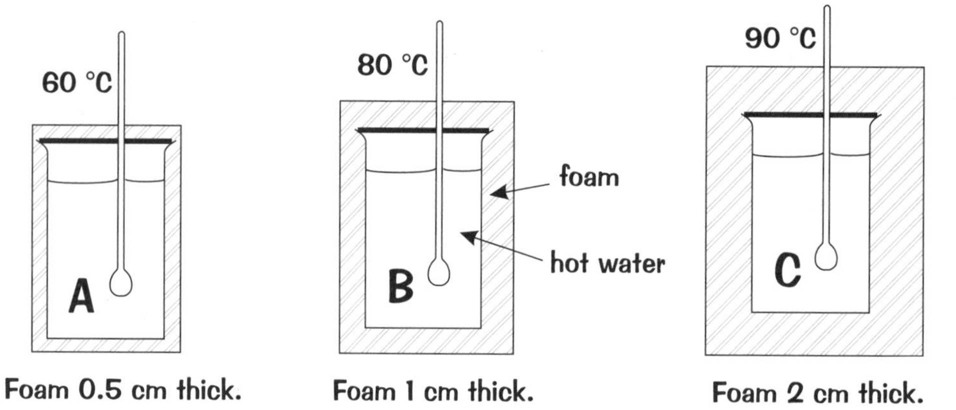

60 °C   80 °C   90 °C

foam

hot water

A   **B**   **C**

Foam 0.5 cm thick.   Foam 1 cm thick.   Foam 2 cm thick.

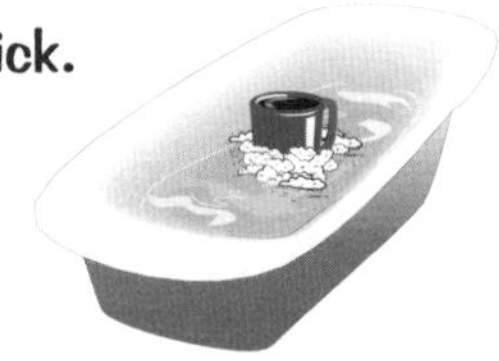

a)   What do Natasha's results tell her?

    ....

    ....

b)   In this experiment, what was:

> This is the thing you *measure*.

i)   the dependent variable? ....

ii) the independent variable? ....

> This is the thing you change.

c)   Natasha's experiment does not include a **control** beaker.
What should she have used as a control, and how would this be useful?

    ....

    ....

Useful Heat Transfers

Q3 Mr Green makes a **solar hot water panel** from an old white central heating radiator made of **steel**.

wooden support
old radiator
wooden roof
air space
pipes connected to hot water tank and pump

Mr Green fixes the panel to the roof of his garden shed. Sadly, he finds that the water does not get very hot, even on sunny days.

Explain how Mr Green could improve the design of his solar hot water panel.

....

....

....

....

Q4 Mr Pink has a copper hot water tank with an electric **immersion heater** in it. The hot water tank **loses heat** from its **walls** by radiation, conduction and convection.

a) Describe one **useful** heat transfer that takes place in the hot water tank.

....

b) Complete the table below, showing how to **reduce non-useful** heat transfers from the tank's walls.

Type of Transfer	Suggested improvements to reduce heat loss
Radiation	
Conduction	
Convection	

Which fluid will move and carry heat away?
Where will it go, and how could you stop it?

Top Tips: Clever people don't wear thick jumpers when it's cold out. Oh no. They put on two thinnish jumpers — to **trap air** between the layers and reduce their heat losses by convection and conduction. Then, they wrap themselves in tinfoil — to reduce their heat losses by radiation.

Energy Transfer

Q1 Complete the following **energy transfer diagrams**. The first one has been done for you.

A solar water heating panel: ....light energy........... → ....heat energy...........

a) A gas cooker: .... → ....heat energy...........

b) An electric buzzer: ....electrical energy........... → ....

c) A television screen: .... → ....

Q2 Use the words below to fill in the gaps.

    conservation   run out   stay the same   resources   principle

The word .... has two very different meanings related to energy.

It can mean using fewer energy .... so that they don't

.... It can also mean the .... that the total

amount of energy in the Universe will always ....

Q3 The diagram shows a **steam locomotive**.

a) What form(s) of energy are there in the:

 i) coal ....

 ii) hot steam (which powers the engine) ....

b) Describe two **energy transfers** which take place on the locomotive.

 1. ....

 2. ....

Q4 Bruce is practising weightlifting.

a) When Bruce holds the bar still, above his head, what kind of energy does the weight have?

....

b) Bruce had porridge for breakfast. Describe how the chemical energy in his porridge is converted to the gravitational potential energy of the lifted bar.

....

....

c) When Bruce lets go of the weight, what happens to its energy?

....

Efficiency of Machines

Q1 Fill in the gaps using the correct words from the list below.

| heat | light | input | create | output | total | useful | fraction | convert |

A **machine** is a device which can .... energy. Some of the energy

supplied to the machine is converted into .... output energy.

But some energy is always wasted — often as .... energy.

The **efficiency** of a **machine** is the .... of the **total energy**

.... that is converted into useful energy ....

Q2 Here is an **energy flow diagram** for an electric lamp. Complete the following sentences.

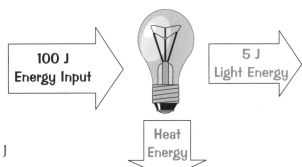

a) The **total energy input** is .... J

b) The **useful energy output** is .... J

c) The amount of energy **wasted** is .... J

Q3 Use the **efficiency formula** to complete the table.

Efficiency = Useful Energy Output ÷ Energy Input

Total Energy Input (J)	Useful Energy Output (J)	Efficiency
2000	1500	
	2000	0.50
4000		0.25
600	200	

Q4 Tina was investigating a model **winch** — a machine that uses an electric motor to lift objects.

Tina calculated that, in theory, **10 J** of electrical energy would be needed to lift a **boot** 50 cm off a table. She then tried lifting the boot with the winch, and found that, actually, **20 J** of electrical energy was used.

Why did the winch use so much electrical energy in practice?
In your answer, include an explanation of what happened to the 'extra' 10 joules.

....

....

Efficiency of Machines

Q5   Sajid hopes his new MP3 player is better than his old one.
He decides to test which one is more **efficient**.

He puts new batteries in both MP3 players
and switches them on. Then he times how long
they each play for before the batteries run out.

a)   Why does Sajid use new batteries?

....

b)   How can he measure the **useful energy outputs**?

....

c)   Write down one thing Sajid must do to make it a **fair test**.

....

d)   Player A lasts for 3 hours and Player B lasts for 4 hours. Write a **conclusion** for Sajid's experiment.

....

Q6   Clive is researching different kinds of electric light bulb. He finds the following information.

	Low-energy bulb	Ordinary bulb
Electrical energy input per second (J)	15	60
Light energy output per second (J)	1.4	1.4
Cost	£3.50	50p
Typical expected lifetime	8 years	1 year
Estimated annual running cost	£1.00	£4.00

*Hint — most people
don't like wasting money.*

a)   Write down two reasons for choosing a **low-energy** light bulb.

1) ....

2) ....

b)   Write down two reasons why Clive might prefer to buy an ordinary bulb.

1) ....

2) ....

Top Tips: There's often more to choosing a light bulb in real life. For example, you
might put an ordinary bulb in a room you rarely use, because the running costs would be so tiny
that any savings would never pay back the extra cost of buying a low-energy bulb.

Efficiency of Machines

Q7 Electric kettles have an **electric heater** which heats the water.
Mr and Mrs Bennett had an argument about their new electric kettle.

Mr Bennett says: "Electric heaters like this one are 100% efficient — they never waste energy."
Mrs Bennett says: "There are at least two ways this kettle could **waste** energy."

Say whether Mr and Mrs Bennett are **right** or **wrong** and explain why.

a) Mr Bennett is .... because ....

....

b) Mrs Bennett is .... because ....

....

Q8 True or false?

		True	False
a)	**i)** **Concentrated** energy is more **useful** than spread-out (or low-grade) energy.	☐	☐
	ii) Whenever energy is transferred, some of it becomes less concentrated.	☐	☐
	iii) Electric heaters can be 100% **efficient**.	☐	☐
	iv) When energy is **transferred**, all the heat energy produced is always **wasted**.	☐	☐

b) Write a correction for each false sentence.

....

....

....

Q9 Mrs Smith is choosing a new kettle. She narrows the choice down to the two kettles shown here.

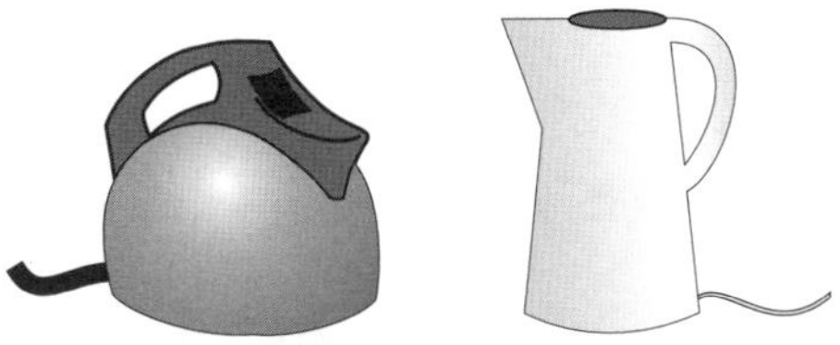

3 litre stainless steel kettle   **2 litre plastic kettle**

Write down five things Mrs Smith should consider when she decides which kettle to buy.

1) ....

2) ....

3) ....

4) ....

5) ....

Energy Transformations

Q1 When an archer shoots an arrow into the air several **energy transformations** take place.
The table below shows these transformations, but in the wrong order.
Number the energy transformations from 1 to 5 to show the correct order.

Order	Energy transformation
	Energy stored in the pulled bow and string is converted into kinetic energy.
	The arrow loses gravitational potential energy and gains kinetic energy as it falls to earth.
	Chemical energy in the archer's muscles is converted into elastic potential energy.
1	Chemical energy from the archer's food is stored in his muscles.
	As it goes upwards the arrow loses kinetic energy and gains gravitational potential energy.

Q2 Sarah eats three slices of **toast and jam** before riding her bicycle to work. Describe the **energy transformations** that take place as Sarah cycles to work.

Don't forget about the energy that's <u>wasted</u>.

....

....

....

....

Q3 Each of the following sentences is incorrect. Write a correct version of each one.

a) In a battery-powered torch, the battery converts **electrical energy** into **light energy**.

....

b) A **wind turbine** converts **kinetic energy** into **electrical energy** only.

....

c) A wind-up toy car converts **chemical** energy into **kinetic energy** and **sound energy**.

....

Q4 Write down the name of a device which converts:

a) electrical energy into **sound energy** ....

b) light energy into **electrical energy** ....

c) electrical energy into **light energy** ....

Physics 1a — Energy and Electricity

Energy Transformation Diagrams

Q1 This diagram shows the energy changes in a **toy crane**. The diagram is drawn to scale.

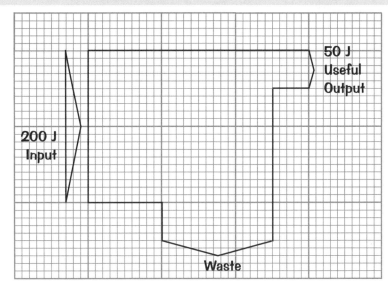

50 J
Useful
Output

200 J
Input

Waste

a) How much energy is **one small square** worth? .... J

b) How much energy is **wasted**? .... J

Q2 Professor Bean is testing a new **high-efficiency** car engine.
He finds that for every 100 J of energy supplied to the engine, 75 J are transformed into **kinetic energy** in the moving car, 5 J are wasted as **sound energy** and the rest is turned into **heat energy**.

On the graph paper below, draw an **energy transformation diagram** to illustrate his results.

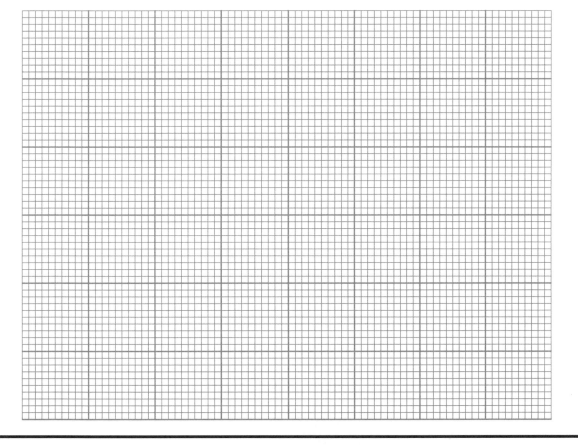

Energy Transformation Diagrams

Q3 Liam measured the energy input and outputs for a model **electrical generator**.
He drew this diagram to show his results.

Describe two mistakes Liam has made on his diagram, and suggest how to correct them.

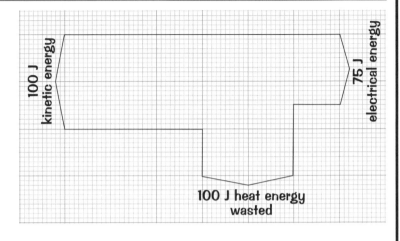

1. ....

....

....

2. ....

....

Q4 The Sankey diagram below is for a **winch** — a machine which **lifts** objects on hooks and cables.

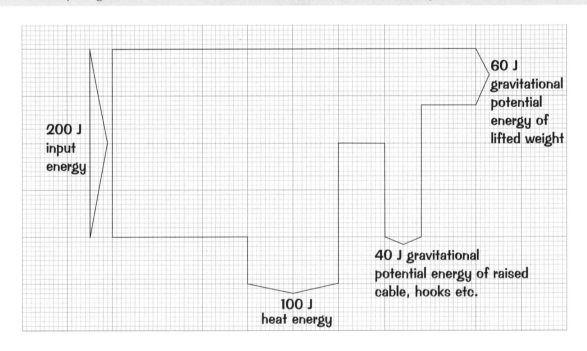

a) What is the total amount of energy **wasted**? .... J

b) How much useful **gravitational energy** is produced? .... J

c) Calculate the **efficiency** of the winch. Give your answer as a decimal.

Efficiency = Useful Energy Output ÷ Energy Input

....

....

The Cost of Electricity

Q1 Boris puts his **2 kW** electric heater on for 3 hours.

    a) Calculate how many **kilowatt-hours** of electrical energy the heater uses.

        Energy used = ...

    b) Boris gets his electricity supply from Ivasparkco. They charge 7p per kilowatt-hour. Work out the **cost** of the energy calculated in part (a).

    ....

    ....

Q2 Calculate the cost of using a **100 W** lamp for **10 hours**, if electrical energy costs **11.3p per kWh**.

You need to turn 100 W into kilowatts first.

    ....

    ....

Q3 Tina's mum grumbles at her for leaving a 60 W lamp on overnight — about 9 hours every night. Tina says her mum uses **more energy** by using an 8 kW shower for 15 minutes every day.

Is Tina right? Calculate how much energy each person uses and compare your results.

    ....

    ....

    ....

    ....

Q4 Mr Havel recently received his electricity bill. Unfortunately, he tore off the bottom part to write a shopping list.

    a) How many **kWh** of energy did Mr Havel use in the three months from June to September?

Customer : Havel, V	
Date	Meter Reading
11 06 06	34259
10 09 06	34783
Total Cost @ 9.7p per kWh	

    ....

    b) What would the bill have said for 'total cost'?

    ....

    ....

Energy Efficiency in the Home

Q1   Heat is lost from a house through its **roof**, **walls**, **doors** and **windows**.

through the roof

....

....

through the doors

....

through the walls

....

....

....

a)   In the spaces on the diagram, write down at least one measure that could be taken to reduce heat losses through each part of the house.

b)   Miss Golightly has just bought a new house which has very large windows.
Suggest three ways she could reduce heat loss through the windows of her new house.

1. ....

2. ....

3. ....

Q2   Explain how the following types of insulation work.

a)   Cavity wall insulation ....

....

b)   Loft insulation ....

....

c)   Hot water tank jacket ....

....

Top Tips: If you want to build a new house, there are regulations about making it energy efficient — that's one reason why a lot of new houses have quite small windows. If you live in an old house, you can sometimes get a grant to cover the cost of installing extra insulation.

Physics 1a — Energy and Electricity

Energy Efficiency in the Home

Q3 Mr Tarantino wants to buy **double glazing** for his house, but the salesman tries to sell him insulated window shutters instead. He says it is cheaper and more **cost-effective**.

	Double glazing	Insulated window shutters
Initial Cost	£3000	£1200
Annual Saving	£60	£20
Payback time	50 years	

a) Calculate the **payback time** for insulated shutters and write it in the table.

b) Is the salesman's advice correct? Give reasons for your answer.

....

....

Q4 A **hot water tank jacket** and **thermostatic controls** do not directly prevent 'heat loss' from a house, but they **will** save energy (and therefore money).

a) How can having **thermostatic controls** help to save energy?

....

b) Explain how installing a **hot water tank jacket** would save you money.

....

Q5 Shona, Tim, Meena and Alison are discussing what 'cost-effectiveness' means.

Cost-effectiveness means having a short payback time.

Shona

Cost-effectiveness means getting good value for your money.

Alison

Cost-effectiveness means getting a job done for a low price.

Tim

Cost-effectiveness just means not wasting energy.

Meena

a) Whose explanations do you think are right? Circle their names.

Shona   Alison   Tim   Meena

b) Explain why the method with the shortest payback time is **not** always the best one to choose.

....

....

....

Electricity and the National Grid

Q1   Number these statements 1 to 5 to show the order of the steps that are needed to deliver energy to Mrs Miggins' house so that she can boil the kettle.

	An electrical current flows through power cables across the country.
	Mrs Miggins boils the kettle for tea.
	Electrical energy is generated in power stations.
	The voltage of the supply is raised.
	The voltage of the supply is reduced.

Q2   Using **high voltages** in power cables means you need some **expensive** equipment.

a)   Make a list of the main equipment you need for **high voltage transmission**.

....

....

b)   Explain why it is still **cheaper** to use **high voltages** for transmission.

....

....

....

Q3   Each of the following sentences is incorrect.
Write a correct version of each.

a)   The National Grid transmits energy at **high voltage** and **high current**.

....

b)   Huge **insulators** are needed because the **cables** get so **hot**.

....

c)   A step-up transformer is used to **reduce the voltage** of the supply before electricity is transmitted.

....

d)   Using a **high current** makes sure there is not much energy **wasted**.

....

Top Tips: The National Grid's pretty good, really — we all get electrical energy whenever we want it (mostly). The key thing to remember is the **high voltage**. And remember **why** it's used — high voltage means low current, which means the cables don't get so hot — so less energy is **wasted**.

Non-renewable Energy & Power Stations

Q1 In a power station, there are several steps involved in making electricity. Number these steps in the right order.

☐ Hot steam rushes through a turbine and makes it spin.

☐ Electricity is produced by the spinning generator.

☐ A fossil fuel such as coal is burned to release heat.

☐ The spinning turbine makes the generator spin too.

☐ Water is heated in a boiler and turned to steam.

Q2 Nuclear power stations provide about 20% of the UK's electrical energy.

a) How do uranium and plutonium provide heat energy?

....

b) Why is nuclear power so expensive?

....

....

Q3 Explain what 'non-renewable' means, in terms of energy resources.

....

Q4 Match up each environmental problem below with something that causes it.

Acid rain

Climate change

Dangerous radioactive waste

Spoiling of natural landscapes

Releasing CO_2 by burning fossil fuels

Coal mining

Sulfur dioxide formed by burning oil and coal

Using nuclear power

Q5 Lisa says: "Using nuclear power to make electricity is too dangerous."
Ben says: "Using fossil fuels is even more dangerous in the long run."

Who do you think is right? Explain your answer.

....

....

....

Using Renewable Energy Resources (1)

Q1   Explain what 'renewable' means, in terms of energy resources.

....

Q2   People often object to wind turbines being put up near to where they live.

a)   List three reasons why they might object.

   1) ....

   2) ....

   3) ....

b)   List three arguments in favour of using wind turbines to generate electricity.

   1) ....

   2) ....

   3) ....

Q3   Geoff wanted to find out how much electricity he could generate using a small wind turbine.
          Each night he used a wind-powered generator to charge a battery. On each following day,
          he timed how long the battery could keep a lamp lit. His results are shown in the table below.

Day	Mon	Tues	Wed	Thu	Fri	Sat	Sun
Time lamp stays lit (mins)	45	50	2	25	60	35	42

a)   Why did Geoff time how long the lamp stayed lit?

....

b)   Suggest a reason why the lamp only stayed lit for 2 minutes on Wednesday.

....

Q4   Explain the advantages and disadvantages of using **solar cells** to
          generate electricity.

....

....

....

Using Renewable Energy Resources (2)

Q1 Lynn and Hua are using the apparatus below to investigate how hydroelectric power works.

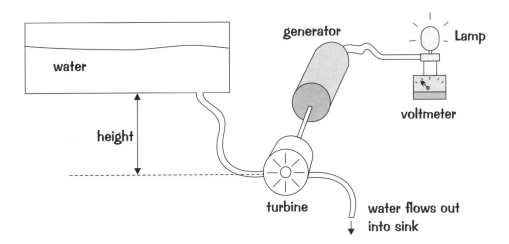

They put the tank at several different heights and recorded the voltage from the generator.

Height of tank (cm)	300	250	200	150	100
Voltage (V)	3.1	2.0	1.1	0.6	0.2
Brightness of lamp	bright	normal	dim	just lit	not lit

a) Why did they measure the **voltage** instead of just noting the brightness of the lamp?

....

b) They predicted that the energy generated would be **proportional** to the height of the tank. Do their results support this prediction? Explain your answer.

Their results **support / do not support** their prediction because ....

....

c) Why do you think the **voltage** was higher when the **tank** was higher?

....

Q2 These sentences explain how pumped storage works. Put them in the right order by numbering them 1 to 4.

☐ Water at a high level stores energy until it is needed.

☐ At peak times, water is allowed to flow downhill, powering turbines and generating electricity.

☐ At night big power stations make more electricity than is needed.

☐ Spare electricity is used to pump water from reservoirs at a low level to others at a high level.

Using Renewable Energy Resources (2)

Q3   Match up the beginnings and ends of the sentences. In one case, two matches are possible.

Big coal-fired power stations deliver energy...

when it is needed.

Pumped storage power stations deliver energy...

all the time.

Hydroelectric power stations deliver electricity...

that they have previously stored.

Q4   At a public meeting, people are sharing their views about hydroelectric power.

We should use hydroelectric power more — it doesn't cause any pollution.

And it gives us loads of free energy.

But it makes a terrible mess of the countryside.

At least it's reliable — it always gives us electricity when we need it.

Brian   **Hillary**   **Sue**   **Liz**

Say whether you agree or disagree with each person's view, and explain your reasons.

a)   I **agree / disagree** with Brian because ....

....

b)   I **agree / disagree** with Hillary because ....

....

c)   I **agree / disagree** with Sue because ....

....

d)   I **agree / disagree** with Liz because ....

....

e)   Outline two **advantages** of hydroelectric power which were not mentioned at the public meeting.

1) ....

2) ....

f)   Outline two **disadvantages** of hydroelectric power not mentioned at the meeting.

1) ....

2) ....

Using Renewable Energy Resources (3)

Q1 Tick the boxes to show whether each statement applies to **wave** power or **tidal** power or **both**.

Wave Tidal

a) Is usually used in estuaries. ☐ ☐

b) Suitable for small-scale use. ☐ ☐

c) Is a reliable way to generate electricity. ☐ ☐

d) The amount of energy generated depends on the weather. ☐ ☐

e) The amount of energy generated depends on the time of the month and year. ☐ ☐

Q2 **Tidal barrages** can be used to generate electricity.

What happens to make turbines go round?

a) Explain how a tidal barrage works.

....

....

....

b) Give two reasons why people might object to a tidal barrage being built.

1. ....

2. ....

Q3 **Wave-powered generators** can be very useful around islands, like Britain.

a) Number these sentences 1 to 6, to explain how a wave-powered generator works.

☐ The spinning generator makes electricity.

☐ The moving air makes the turbine spin.

☐ The water goes down again.

☐ Air is sucked downwards, spinning the turbine the other way and generating more power.

☐ A wave moves water upwards, forcing air out towards a turbine.

☐ The spinning turbine drives a generator.

b) Give two possible problems with using wave power.

1. ....

2. ....

Using Renewable Energy Resources (4)

Q1 Explain why:

a) Some rocks underground are very hot. ....

....

b) Biomass is a 'renewable' source of energy. ....

....

c) Burning biomass is 'carbon neutral'. ....

....

Q2 Mr Saleem is a cattle farmer in India. He has just installed a small **biogas** plant on his farm.

a) What source of biogas is Mr Saleem likely to use?

....

b) Apart from cooking and heating, how could Mr Saleem make use of the biogas?

....

Q3 Tick the correct boxes to show whether these statements apply to generating electricity from **geothermal** energy, **biomass** or **both**.

	Biomass	Geothermal
a) Set-up costs are low.	☐	☐
b) Does not release CO_2.	☐	☐
c) Possible in any country in the world.	☐	☐
d) Reduces the need for landfill sites.	☐	☐

Q4 Fiza and Julie are discussing the environmental impacts of burning landfill rubbish to generate electricity.

Fiza says: **"Burning rubbish gives off harmful gases."**

Julie says: **"But it's better than just burying your rubbish and burning coal instead."**

Who do you think is right? Explain your answer.

....

....

Top Tips: Burning animal poo is nothing new — people have been doing it for years, and many still do. For instance, if you're a nomadic yak herder in Mongolia, you probably don't have **mains electricity**, but you **do** have lots of **yak poo**. Dry it, burn it, and you'll have a nice warm tent.

Comparison of Energy Resources

Q1 The city of Fakeville decides to replace its old coal-fired power station.
They have to choose between using gas, nuclear, wind or biomass.

Give one **disadvantage** of each choice:

a) **Gas** ....

   ....

b) **Nuclear** ....

   ....

c) **Wind** ....

   ....

d) **Biomass** ....

   ....

Q2 This is part of a leaflet produced by the pressure group 'Nuclear Is Not the Answer' (NINA).

Read the extract and answer the questions on the next page.

Imagine life without electricity. No lights, no computers, no TV… no kettles, no tea? Unthinkable. But that's what could happen when the oil and gas run out — because in the UK we generate about 80% of our electricity from power stations running on fossil fuels.

The Government is considering whether we should build more nuclear power stations. At NINA, we believe that nuclear is not the answer.

Nuclear power stations generate power, yes, but they also generate huge piles of highly radioactive waste. No one has any idea how to get rid of this waste safely. So should we really be making more of it? Radioactive waste stays dangerous for hundreds of thousands of years. Would you be happy living near a nuclear fuel dump? That's not all — nuclear power stations, and the lethal waste they create, are obvious targets for terrorists. And, last but not least, building more nuclear power stations would cost the taxpayer billions.

The good news is, we don't need nuclear power. There are safer, cleaner ways to produce electricity — using renewable energy. Many people argue that renewables are unreliable — the wind doesn't always blow, for instance. Well, true, but tidal power is reliable — and we have hundreds of miles of coastline with tides washing in and out twice every day.

There's still time. If you don't want your children to grow up in a nuclear-powered world, join NINA today.

Comparison of Energy Resources

a) Explain clearly why the author thinks that we could find ourselves without electricity.

....

....

b) Give two reasons why the author thinks nuclear power is **dangerous**.

1. ....

....

2. ....

....

c) Apart from safety concerns, why else does the author feel that nuclear power is a bad choice?

....

d) The author suggests that tidal power is a **plentiful** and **reliable** source of energy. Do you agree? Explain your answer.

I **agree** / **disagree** because

....

....

....

....

e) Give two possible arguments **in favour** of nuclear power.

1. ....

....

2. ....

....

<u>Mixed Questions — Physics 1a</u>

Q1   Explain:

a)   how a layer of **snow** can stop young plants dying in the **frost**.

....

b)   how cavity wall insulation works.

....

c)   why birds try to keep warm in winter by **ruffling** up their feathers.

....

d)   why, in winter, **cloudy** nights are usually **warmer** than clear nights.

....

....

Q2   Ben sets up an experiment as shown.
He records the temperature readings on
thermometers A and B every two minutes.

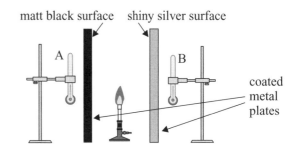

The graph below shows Ben's results
for thermometer **B**.

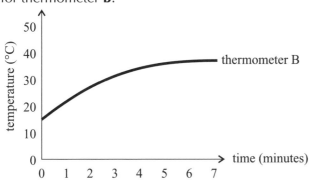

a)   On the diagram above, sketch the graph you would expect for thermometer **A**.

b)   Explain why the differences between the two graphs occur.

....

....

Q3   Fridge-freezers often have their freezer compartment above the refrigerator.
How does this arrangement encourage **convection currents** in the main body of the fridge?

....

....

Mixed Questions — Physics 1a

Q4   Jemima is sanding some floorboards with an **electric sander** which has a power rating of **360 W**. Jemima has the sander on for **45 minutes**.

a)   How many kWh of electrical energy does the sander use in this time?

....

b)   If the sander is only **55% efficient**, how many **joules** of energy are **wasted**?

....

....

c)   Jemima's electricity supplier charges **14.8p per kWh**. What will be the cost of the 'wasted' energy? (Give your answer to the nearest penny.)

....

Q5   In one gas-fired power station, for every **1000 J** of energy input to the power station, 100 J is wasted in the **boiler**, 500 J is wasted in the **cooling water** and 50 J is wasted in the **generator**.

a)   What **type** of energy is contained in the **coal**? ....

b)   On the grid below, draw a detailed energy transformation diagram for this power station.

c)   Calculate the **efficiency** of the power station. ....

d)   Electricity generated in power stations reaches our homes by a network of power cables. Explain:

   i)   why these power cables are at very high voltages ....

   ....

   ii)   why the high voltage is not dangerous for people using the electricity ....

   ....

Mixed Questions — Physics 1a

Q6   Eric investigates ways of saving energy in his grandmother's house. He calculates the annual savings that could be made on his grandma's fuel bills, and the cost of doing the work.

Work needed	Annual Saving (£)	Cost of work (£)
Hot water tank jacket	15	15
Draught-proofing	65	70
Cavity wall insulation	70	560
Thermostatic controls	25	120

a)   Which of these energy-saving measures has the shortest **payback time**?

....

b)   Which of the options in the table would save Eric's grandma the most money **over 5 years**? Show your working.

....

....

....

c)   Eric's grandma has an open fire which burns **logs**. Eric tells her this is an inefficient way to heat the house, and says she should have a **gas fire**. She says that burning natural gas is more environmentally damaging than burning logs. Is she right? Explain your answer.

....

....

....

Q7   A group of farmers live on a remote island, growing potatoes and farming llamas. They decide to put **solar cells** on the roofs of their houses and put up **wind turbines** in their fields.

a)   Suggest why the farmers have chosen to use:

i) solar power ....

....

ii) wind power ....

....

b)   What other renewable sources of energy could the farmers use?

....

Electromagnetic Waves

Q1 Diagrams A, B and C represent electromagnetic waves.

A   **B**   **C**

a) Which two diagrams show waves with the same **frequency**? ...... and ......

b) Which two diagrams show waves with the same **amplitude**? ...... and ......

c) Which two diagrams show waves with the same **wavelength**? ...... and ......

Q2 Indicate whether the following statements are true or false.

True   False

a) Visible light travels faster in a vacuum than both X-rays and radio waves. ☐ ☐

b) All EM waves transfer matter from place to place. ☐ ☐

c) Radio waves have the shortest wavelength of all EM waves. ☐ ☐

d) All EM waves can travel through space. ☐ ☐

Q3 Red and violet are at opposite ends of the spectrum of **visible** light.
Describe two things they have in common and two ways in which they differ.

....

....

....

....

Q4 EM waves with higher frequencies are generally more damaging. Explain, in terms of wavelength and frequency, why some **ultraviolet** radiation can be almost as damaging as **X-rays**.

....

....

Q5 **Green light** travels at 3×10^8 m/s and has a wavelength of about 5×10^{-7} m.

Calculate the **frequency** of green light. Give the correct unit in your answer.

You'll have to use $v = f\lambda$.

....

....

Electromagnetic Waves

Q6 The house shown below receives radio signals from a nearby transmitter, even though there is a mountain between the house and the transmitter.

radio transmitter

Use the words below to fill in the blanks in the passage.

ionosphere   direct current   short-wave   long-wave   alternating current   absorbs   reflects

The house can receive .... signals because they can bend

around the mountain. It also receives .... signals

because they are reflected by the .... A radio has an

aerial which .... the EM waves and changes them into an

....

Q7 The diagrams show the arrangement of atoms in a dense material and in a less dense material.

dense material

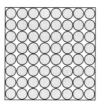

less dense material

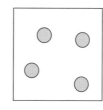

Dense materials are more likely to **reflect** or **absorb** electromagnetic waves. **Less dense** materials are more likely to transmit them.

Try drawing a ray of light hitting the material. How likely is it to hit an atom (and what happens to its energy when it does?)

Explain why this is.

....

....

....

Top Tips: **Absorption** of EM radiation can cause **heating** (useful in ovens) and/or an **alternating current** (useful in radios etc.). Radiation isn't always absorbed though — it could be reflected or transmitted. This depends on **what** the material is, and the **wavelength** of the radiation.

Electromagnetic Waves

Q8 Materials X, Y and Z were tested to see how well they transmit electromagnetic radiation. Detector B was used to measure what percentage of the energy emitted (from A) reached it.

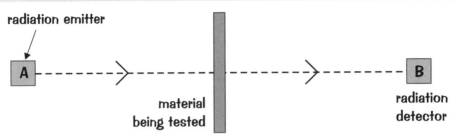

radiation emitter

material
being tested

radiation
detector

The table shows the results of the test.

a) **i)** Which material **transmitted** most of the energy that was directed at it? ....

ii) What may have happened to the energy that was **not** detected at B when this material was tested?

Material	Detector B (%)
X	0
Y	90
Z	50

....

....

b) **No energy** reached detector B when sample X was tested.
What conclusions can you draw from this result? Tick the boxes next to any valid conclusions.

☐ Sample X absorbed all the energy that was directed at it.

☐ Sample X reflected all the energy that was directed at it.

☐ Sample X would be a poor choice of material for using in windows

c) State **three** things which must be kept the same in this experiment to make it a fair test.

....

Q9 Indicate whether each statement is **true** or **false**.

		True	False
a)	Some electromagnetic waves can kill cells in the body.	☐	☐
b)	All electromagnetic waves are absorbed by the body.	☐	☐
c)	The harm done by EM radiation depends on its wavelength (or frequency) only.	☐	☐

Q10 Explain why:

a) Electric fires glow red, even though infrared radiation (heat radiation) is invisible to the human eye.

....

b) UV tubes glow blue, even though UV radiation is invisible to the human eye.

....

Microwaves and Infrared

Q1   Microwaves are used for **cooking** as well as for mobile phone **communications**.

Explain why your body does not get 'cooked' when you use a mobile phone.

....

....

Q2   Explain how a microwave camera on a remote-sensing satellite can 'see' through clouds.

....

....

Q3   Gabrielle in Britain and Carwyn in Canada are talking by mobile phone.

Communications Satellite

NOT TO SCALE

Gabrielle's phone

Carwyn's phone

Atlantic Ocean

a)   The distance from phone to phone, via the satellite, is approximately 6000 km. How long will it take the signal from Gabrielle's phone to arrive at Carwyn's phone?

....

....

....

b)   The signal from a mobile phone gets weaker with distance. How is this problem overcome?

....

....

c)   Suggest why the satellite needs to be high above the Earth.

....

....

Microwaves and Infrared

Q4   A **cable TV** company uses a large dish to collect TV signals from a satellite in space.
It then sends these signals to houses along **optical fibres**.

a)   What type(s) of EM waves could be used to send the signals along the optical fibres?

....

b)   Give three advantages of using optical fibres to transmit signals, rather than broadcasting them.

....

....

....

Q5   Doctors can use an **endoscope** to look inside
a patient's body. An endoscope has two bundles
of optical fibres — one carries light down into
your stomach, say, and the other returns the
reflected light back to a monitor.

a)   What material could the optical fibres
in the endoscope be made from?

....

b)   Optical fibres work because of repeated **total internal reflections**.

i)   Complete the ray diagrams below. The critical angle for glass/air is 42°.

You'll need to measure the angle of incidence for each one — carefully.

ii)   What two conditions are essential for total internal reflection to occur?

....

....

c)   Explain why doctors must be careful not to **bend** an endoscope sharply.

....

....

Microwaves and Infrared

Read this extract about the safety of microwave ovens.

Microwave ovens are designed to generate microwaves to heat up food. So should we be worried that microwaves are cooking us, as well as our dinner?

Well, probably not. The Microwave Technologies Association, which represents manufacturers, stresses that microwave ovens are lined with metal to stop microwaves getting out, and that there are regulations about how much 'leakage' is allowed. They also point out that the intensity of leaked radiation decreases rapidly with distance from the oven. So don't press your nose to the glass to watch your chicken korma reheating — gaze from a distance.

We can't be certain that microwave ovens are absolutely safe — there might be long-term health problems that no one's spotted yet. But perhaps we should be more worried about other uses of microwave technology, like mobile phones. Mobile phones use microwaves — though of a lower frequency than those used in ovens. But mobile phones are very definitely *designed* to emit microwaves (or else they wouldn't work) — so are they silently 'cooking' our brains?

Interestingly, my mobile phone can still make calls from inside a microwave oven, with the door shut. If the microwaves from my phone are powerful enough to get out of the oven — with all its fancy shielding — then what on earth are they doing to my brain?

a) Why might it be a serious health hazard if microwaves 'leak' from microwave ovens?

....

....

....

b) According to the article, microwave ovens have a **metal lining** to stop microwaves getting out. This suggests that microwaves may be (circle any which apply):

    A   absorbed by the metal lining

    B   reflected by the metal lining

    C   transmitted by the metal lining

Microwaves and Infrared

c) Why does the article advise you not to "press your nose to the glass" of a microwave oven? Circle the correct answer.

    A   because the radiation from microwave ovens is known to cause cancer

    B   because some radiation may be "leaking" from the oven

    C   to avoid bruising

    D   because you might burn your skin

d) Why does keeping your distance from a microwave oven reduce the chance that you will suffer harmful effects from it?

....

....

e) Why does the article mention that the Microwave Technologies Association represents manufacturers?

....

....

f) Mobile phones also emit microwaves when you are making a call.

    i) Do the microwaves emitted by **mobile phones** have a longer or shorter **wavelength** than those used in ovens? Circle the correct answer.

                longer   shorter

    ii) Why does the author think we should be more concerned about the ill effects of microwaves from mobile phones than from microwave ovens?

....

....

Top Tips: People love a good scare story. Microwave ovens are **probably** perfectly safe. Mobile phones haven't been around for so long, so it's difficult to know if they're doing us any long-term harm. You could say, though, that it's safer to stay at home, heating up ready meals in the microwave and making calls on your mobile, than it is to cross a busy, fume-choked city street to find a phone box or go to the pizza shop. Watch out for the salt in those ready meals, though.

Hazards of EM Radiation

Q1   Choose from the words below to complete this passage.

lead   plastic   bones   transmitted   soft tissue   aluminium   absorbed

X-rays can pass easily through .... but are ....

more by .... Screens and shields made of

.... are used to minimise unnecessary exposure to X-rays.

Q2   Give two examples of how EM waves can be **helpful** and two examples of how they can be **harmful**.

Helpful: 1) .... 2) ....

Harmful: 1) .... 2) ....

Q3   The graph opposite shows how the **energy** of EM waves varies with **frequency**.

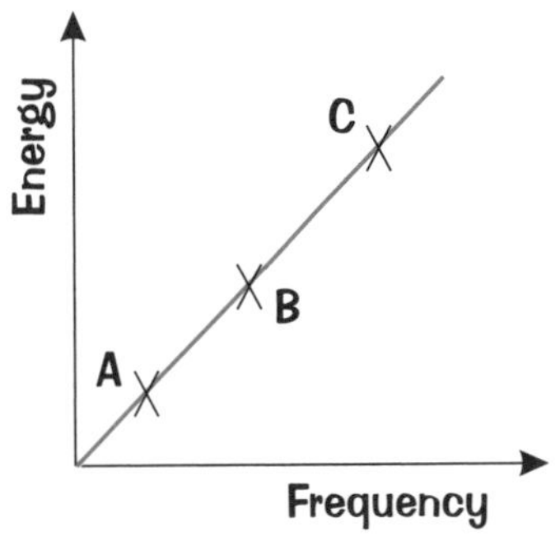

a)   What is the mathematical relationship between frequency and energy?

....

....

b)   Draw arrows to match points **A**, **B** and **C** on the graph to the three types of radiation below.

green light	gamma radiation	radio waves
A	B	C

Q4   Explain why:

a)   It is safe to use fluorescent tubes in lights, even though harmful UV rays are produced inside them.

....

b)   Darker-skinned people are less likely to suffer from skin cancer.

....

....

c)   Radiographers stand behind lead screens when they are taking X-rays of a patient, even though it's considered an acceptable risk for the patient to be deliberately exposed to X-rays.

....

....

Analogue and Digital Signals

Q1 Fill in the blanks, using the words below.

| analogue | digital | analogue | amplified | weaken | interference | noise |

All signals .... as they travel. To overcome this, they can be

.... Signals may also suffer .... from

other signals or from electrical disturbances. This causes ....

in the signal. When .... signals are amplified, the noise is

also amplified.

Q2 Sketch: a 'clean' digital signal.   a 'noisy' digital signal.   a 'noisy' analogue signal.

Q3 a) Explain why it is better to send **digital** signals to a computer rather than analogue ones.

....

b) Explain why digital signals suffer less from **noise** than analogue signals.

....

....

c) State one other advantage of using digital signals for communication.

....

Q4 The diagrams opposite show magnified views of the surfaces of a **compact disc** and an old-fashioned **record**.

The CD is 'read' by a laser, along the path shown by the arrow. The record is read by a needle which follows the grooves.

Both devices produce an electrical signal, which is then converted into sound.

For each device, sketch the type of trace you would expect to see on a monitor.

Compact disc

Old-fashioned record

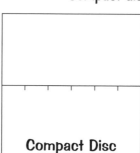

Compact Disc

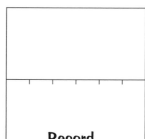

Record

Radioactivity

Q1 Fill in the blanks using the words below. Each word should be used only once.

| radiation | isotope | element | protons | neutrons | nuclei | radioactive |

Isotopes are atoms which have the same number of ....

but different numbers of .... Some isotopes are

.... Their .... are unstable, so they

break down and spit out .... When this happens the

nucleus often changes into a new ....

Q2 Carbon-14 is radioactive but carbon-12 is not.
Explain why, in terms of the difference between their **nuclei**.

....

....

Q3 Indicate whether these sentences are **true** or **false**.

True **False**

a) The nucleus of an atom takes up almost no space compared to the whole atom. ☐ ☐

b) Most of an atom's mass is in the electrons. ☐ ☐

c) Atoms of the same element with the same number of neutrons are called isotopes. ☐ ☐

d) Radioactive decay speeds up at higher temperatures. ☐ ☐

Q4 In a famous experiment Sir Ernest Rutherford got his students to aim a stream of **alpha particles** at a piece of **gold foil**. They noticed that most of the particles went straight through, unaffected in any way, but a few changed direction.

gold foil · alpha particles

a) What had happened to the particles which changed direction?

....

....

b) What idea about the **nucleus** is supported by these results?

....

....

Radioactivity

Q5 Complete the passage using the words given below. You will not have to use all the words.

ions   less   more   electrons   further   less far   protons

When ionising radiation hits atoms it sometimes knocks ....

off the atoms and makes them into .... Radiations that are

more ionising travel .... into a material and tend to cause

.... damage in the material they have penetrated.

Q6 Complete the table below by choosing the correct word from each column.

Radiation Type	Ionising power weak/moderate/ strong	Charge positive/none/ negative	Relative mass no mass/ small/large	Penetrating power low/moderate/ high	Relative speed slow/fast/ very fast
alpha					
beta					
gamma					

Q7 a) For each sentence, tick the correct box to show whether it is **true** or **false**.

True **False**

i) All nuclear radiation is deflected by magnetic fields. ☐ ☐

ii) Gamma radiation has no mass because it is an EM wave. ☐ ☐

iii) Alpha is the slowest and most strongly ionising type of radiation. ☐ ☐

iv) Beta particles are electrons, so they do not come from the nucleus. ☐ ☐

b) For each of the false sentences, write out a correct version.

....

....

....

Radioactivity

Q8 Radiation from three sources — A, B and C — was directed through an **electric field** (between X and Y), towards target sheets of **paper**, **aluminium** and **lead**. Counters were used to detect where radiation passed through the target sheets.

Source A — the radiation was partially absorbed by the lead.
Source B — the radiation was deflected by the electric field, and stopped by the paper.
Source C — the radiation was deflected by the electric field, and stopped by the aluminium.

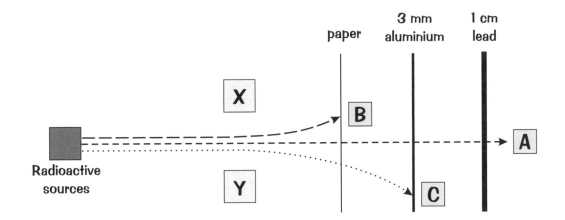

a) What type of radiation is emitted by:

source A? ...., source B? ...., source C? ....

b) Explain why source A is **not deflected** by the electric field.

....

....

c) What other type of **field** would deflect radiation from sources B and C? ....

Q9 Explain clearly why gamma rays are **less ionising** than alpha particles.

....

....

....

Top Tips: Alpha, beta and gamma radiation are different **things** and they also have different **properties**. You need to understand how they vary in ionising power, penetrating power, speed etc.

Physics 1b — Radiation and the Universe

Half-life

Q1   A radioactive isotope has a half-life of 60 years.
Which of these statements describes this isotope correctly? Tick one box only.

In 60 years half of the atoms in the material will have gone. ☐

In 30 years' time only half the atoms will be radioactive. ☐

In 60 years' time the count rate will be half what it is now. ☐

In about 180 years there will be almost no radioactivity left in the material. ☐

Q2   The graph shows how the count rate of a radioactive isotope declines with time.

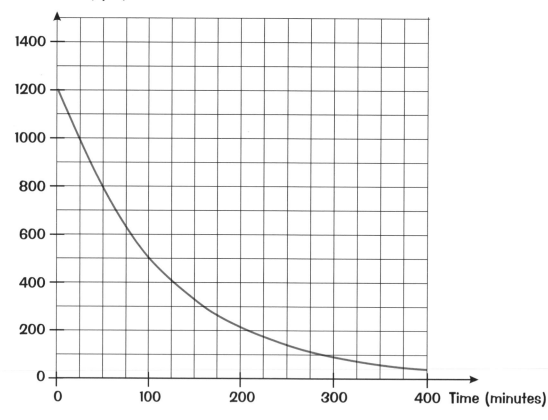

a)   What is the half-life of this isotope? ....

b)   What was the count rate after 3 half-lives? ....

c)   What fraction of the original radioactive nuclei will still be unstable after 5 half-lives?

....

d)   After how long was the count rate down to 100? ....

Half-life

Q3   The half-life of uranium-238 is 4500 million years. The half-life of carbon-14 is 5730 years.

a)   What do the '238' in "uranium-238" and the '14' in "carbon-14" mean?

....

....

b)   If you start with a sample of each element and the two samples
have equal activity, which will lose its radioactivity first?
Circle the correct answer.

uranium-238   carbon-14

Q4   A radioactive isotope has a half-life of 40 seconds.

You'll need to change 6 minutes into underline seconds.

a)   What fraction of the unstable nuclei will still be radioactive after 6 minutes?

....

....

b)   **i)**   If the initial count rate of the sample was 8000 counts per minute,
what would be the approximate count rate after 6 minutes?

....

....

ii)   After how many whole **minutes** would the count rate have fallen below 10 counts per minute?

....

....

Q5   Peter was trying to explain half-life to his little brother. He said, "isotopes with a long half-life
are always more dangerous than those with a short half-life."

Is Peter right? Explain your answer.

....

....

....

Top Tips: Half-life tells you **how quickly** a source becomes **less radioactive**. If your source
has a half-life of 50 years then after 100 years the count rate will be 1/4 of its original value. But if
the half-life's 10 years, after 100 years the count rate will be less than 1/1000th of its original value.

Physics 1b — Radiation and the Universe

Uses of Radiation

Q1 The table shows the **properties** needed for different uses of radioactivity, and the **types** of radioactive sources that are used.

Choose the appropriate words to complete the table (some have been done for you).

Use of radiation	Penetrating power (low/high)	Ionising power (low/high)	Half-life (short/long)	Type of radiation (α, β, γ)
Smoke alarm	Low			
Medical tracers			Short	
Detecting leaks in pipes		Low		

Q2 The following sentences explain how a smoke detector works, but they are in the wrong order.

Put them in order by labelling them 1 (first) to 6 (last).

☐ The circuit is broken so no current flows.

1 The radioactive source emits alpha particles.

☐ A current flows between the electrodes — the alarm stays off.

☐ The alarm sounds.

☐ The air between the electrodes is ionised by the alpha particles.

☐ A fire starts and smoke particles absorb the alpha radiation.

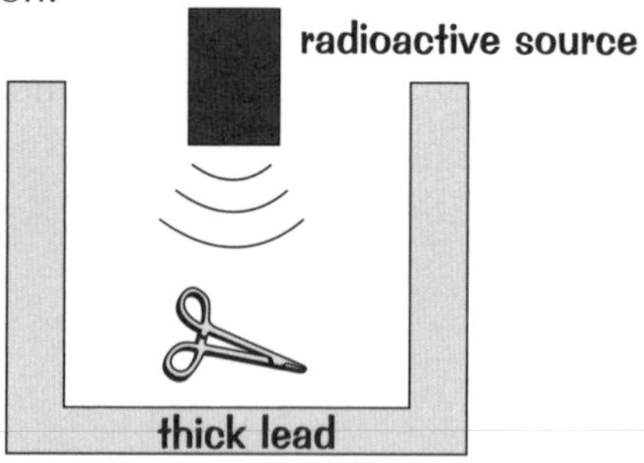

Q3 The diagram shows how radiation can be used to sterilise surgical instruments.

a) What kind of radioactive source is used, and why? In your answer, mention the **type** of radiation emitted (α, β and γ) and the **half-life** of the source.

....

....

b) What is the purpose of the thick lead?

....

c) Similar machines can be used to treat fruit before it is exported from South America to Europe, to stop it going bad on the long journey. How does irradiating the fruit help?

....

....

Uses of Radiation

Q4 Eviloilco knows that its oil pipeline is leaking somewhere between points A and B.

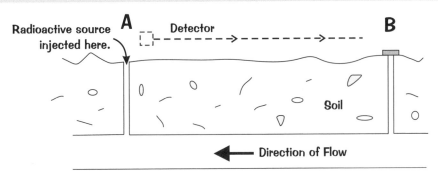

This is how Eviloilco plans to find the leak.

> We will inject a source of alpha radiation into the pipeline at point A. (This source has a long half-life — giving us better value for money in the long term.) After injecting the radioactive material, we will pass a sensor along the surface above the pipeline — and so detect where radiation is escaping, hence pinpointing the leak.

a) Give **two** reasons why Eviloilco has made a bad choice of radioactive source, and describe the type of source they should use.

....

....

....

b) Even if they use the correct type of radioactive source, their plan will still fail. Why?

....

Q5 A patient has a radioactive source injected into her body to test her kidneys.

A healthy kidney will get rid of the radioactive material quickly (to the bladder). Damaged kidneys take longer to do this.

The results of the test, for both the patient's kidneys, are shown opposite.

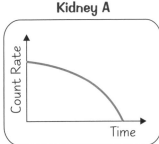

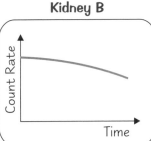

a) Explain how the doctor knew which kidney was working well and which was not.

....

....

b) Explain why an alpha source would **not** be suitable for this investigation.

....

....

Risks from Radiation

Q1   Two scientists are handling samples of radioactive material.

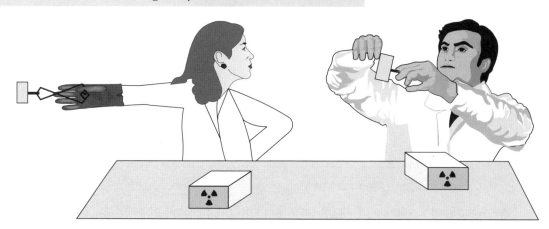

a)   One of the scientists is taking sensible safety precautions, but the other is not.
Describe three things which the careless scientist is doing wrong.

1. ....

2. ....

3. ....

b)   Describe another way the scientists can reduce their exposure to the radiation,
without using special apparatus or clothing.

....

c)   How should radioactive samples be stored when they are not in use?

....

Q2   In industry, highly penetrating radiation sources sometimes need to be moved from place to place.

a)   How can this be done without endangering the workers?

....

b)   Gamma radiation can pass easily through the walls of buildings.
How can workers in the surrounding areas be protected from this hazard?

....

Top Tips: You should always handle radioactive sources really carefully. People who work
with radioisotopes often wear **dosimeters** — badges which record their exposure. We're all exposed
to a low level of **background radiation** every day, though — from rocks etc. — and you can't do
anything about that (unless you fancy wearing a lead-lined suit and breathing apparatus all day long.

Risks from Radiation

Q3   Skin cancers are often surgically removed.
Tumours deeper within the body are often treated by radiotherapy, using **gamma rays**.

a)   How does radiotherapy treat cancer?

....

b)   What properties do gamma rays have which make them suitable for radiotherapy?

....

....

c)   Why is a high dose used?

....

Q4   The three different types of radiation can all be dangerous.

a)   Which **two** types of radiation can pass through the human body?
Circle the correct answers.

           alpha   beta   gamma

b)   **i)**   Which type of radiation is usually most dangerous if it's inhaled or swallowed?

....

ii)   What effects can this type of radiation have on the human body?

....

Q5   In 1986, a nuclear reactor at Chernobyl (in Ukraine) exploded, and a lot of radioactive material
was released. Many people were exposed to high doses of radiation. Since then scientists have
monitored the health of people living in the affected areas.

a)   Why have scientists monitored people's health for so long after the explosion?

Think about half-life and dose.

....

....

b)   The Chernobyl explosion provided scientists with a unique opportunity to study
the **effects** of radiation exposure on **humans**. Why could scientists not study this
by collecting data in a laboratory?

....

....

The Origin of the Universe

Q1 Complete this passage using the words supplied below.

expansion	matter	energy	expand	age	explosion

Many scientists believe that the Universe started with all the

.... and .... in one small space.

There was a huge .... and the material started to

.... Scientists can estimate the .... of

the Universe using the current rate of ....

Q2 Brian set up a microphone at his local railway station to record his favourite **train noises**. He attached the microphone to an oscilloscope.

An express train passed through the station at a constant speed. Diagram A below shows the trace on the monitor at 11:31:07, as the train **approached** Brian's microphone.

On diagram B, sketch the trace Brian might have seen as the train **left** the station.

A
11:31:07

B
11:31:08

Q3 What **evidence** is there to support the idea that the Universe is expanding? Include a brief explanation of **red-shift** in your answer.

....

....

....

....

Q4 The expanding Universe can be likened to the surface of a bubble which is getting bigger.

a) What happens to two "particles" which start off near each other as the bubble expands?

....

b) Some of the material in the Universe actually comes together in galaxies. How can this be explained?

....

....

Looking into Space

Q1 Astronomers can use a number of strategies to improve the quality of the images they get of space from Earth-based telescopes.

a) How can they get good images of **faint**, **distant** objects using optical telescopes?

....

....

....

b) How can they improve an optical telescope's **resolution** (ability to see detail)?

....

....

Q2 The **Hubble Space Telescope** can produce images which are much better than those from any Earth-based optical telescopes of a similar size.

a) Explain why the pictures from the Hubble Telescope are clearer and brighter.

....

....

b) List **three** possible **disadvantages** of using space telescopes.

1. ....

2. ....

3. ....

Q3 Astronomers use various telescopes designed to collect different types of electromagnetic waves. Why do they not just use **optical telescopes** situated on Earth or in space?

....

....

....

Looking into Space

Q4 **Radio telescopes** need to be very large, or else the images are 'fuzzy' and lack detail.

a) Why is this?

....

....

....

b) To produce images with a similar degree of detail, which would need to be **larger** — an infrared telescope or an ultraviolet telescope? Circle the correct answer.

infrared   ultraviolet

Q5 Astronomers can't use X-ray telescopes on Earth.

Explain why this is.

....

....

Q6 Only **one** of these statements about the Hubble Space Telescope is **true**.

Circle A, B, C or D to indicate which statement is correct.

A   It was placed in space in order to get closer to the stars.

B   It is placed in space to avoid problems caused by the atmosphere.

C   It uses radio waves rather than light waves to get a better picture of the stars.

D   It was placed in space so that NASA could use it to spy on Russia.

Top Tips: With telescopes, the rule seems to be 'big is beautiful'. And it's best to think up a good name to make sure everyone knows your telescope's the biggest. There's one in Chile called the Very Large Telescope. Imaginative. Better still, there are plans to build a really big new optical telescope — 100 m across — and call it the Overwhelmingly Large Telescope. Beat that.

Mixed Questions — Physics 1b

Q1   The waves A, B and C represent **infrared**, **visible light** and **ultraviolet** radiation (not in that order).

Tick the box next to any of the following statements which are **true**.

☐ B represents ultraviolet radiation.

☐ The infrared wave has the largest amplitude.

☐ C has the highest frequency.

☐ A has the shortest wavelength.

Q2   Radio Roary transmits **long-wave** signals with a wavelength of **1.5 km**.

a)   Calculate the **frequency** of Radio Roary's transmission. (Use speed = 3×10^8 m/s.)

....

....

b)   Mr Potts is on holiday in the Scottish Highlands. He follows England's progress in the cricket test match on Radio Roary, but he can't watch the coverage on television, because TV reception at the cottage is so poor.

Explain why Mr Potts gets **good** long-wave radio reception, but such **poor** TV reception.

....

....

c)   Radio Piracy broadcasts at a frequency of 201 kHz.
Both Radio Roary and Radio Piracy broadcast **analogue** signals.

i)   Why might this be a problem for people listening to these stations?

....

....

ii)   Suggest a way to reduce the problem without changing the frequency of the transmissions.

....

Q3   My landline telephone is connected to the telephone exchange by **optical fibres**.

a)   What **type** of EM wave might be sent from the exchange? ....

b)   Draw an annotated diagram to show how an optical fibre works.

Mixed Questions — Physics 1b

Q4 Remote-sensing **satellites** can be used to 'see' the Earth from space.
Telescopes can be put in space and used to 'see' other parts of the Universe.

a) Many satellites use microwaves to 'see' the Earth. How are these microwaves different from the microwaves used in ovens, and why is this important?

....

....

b) **i)** In what ways are space telescopes better than Earth-based ones?

....

ii) Some types of telescope will **only** work from space. What kind, and why?

....

Q5 Infrared radiation is used by TV **remote controls**. Jake shows Peter that he can change the TV channel by pointing the remote control at a mirror on the opposite wall.

a) What property of EM rays has Jake demonstrated? Circle the correct answer.

reflection   refraction   diffraction

b) Peter places a dull black piece of card over the mirror and tries to change channel in the same way. Explain what will happen now and why.

....

....

Q6 Cancer is sometimes treated using **gamma rays**.

a) When any substance **absorbs** EM radiation, what two effects can happen?

....

b) Explain why patients treated with **gamma** rays can feel very ill.

....

c) Cancer can be **caused** as well as treated by exposure to EM radiation.

i) Which types of EM radiation are known to cause cancer?

....

ii) State and explain the link between the frequency of EM radiation and how dangerous it is.

....

....

Mixed Questions — Physics 1b

Q7 The table gives information about four different **radioisotopes**.

Source	Type of Radiation	Half-life
radon-222	alpha	3.8 days
technetium-99m	gamma	6 hours
americium-241	alpha	432 years
cobalt-60	beta and gamma	5.27 years

a) Explain how the atomic structure of cobalt-60 is different from the structure of 'normal' cobalt-59.

....

b) Which sources in the table would be most suitable for each of the uses below?

   medical tracers   smoke detectors   detecting leaks in pipes

....

c) Jim measures the count rate of a sample of americium-241 as 120 cpm.
Roughly how long would it take for the count rate to fall below **4 cpm**? Show your working.

....

....

d) Explain how nuclear radiation can cause **ionisation**.

....

....

Q8 The diagram represents a **light wave** emitted by a distant galaxy.

a) On the diagram, redraw the wave to show how it might appear to us on Earth because the light is **red-shifted**.

b) Explain how red-shifts from distant and nearer galaxies provide evidence for the Big Bang theory.

....

....

....

Q9 Why do astronomers often want to make telescopes as **big** as possible?

....

....

Physics 2(i) — Forces and Motion

Velocity and Acceleration

Q1　A pulse of laser light takes 1.3 seconds to travel from the Moon to the Earth. The speed of light is approximately 3×10^8 m/s

You'll need to rearrange the speed formula.

How far away is the Moon from the Earth? Give your answer in km.

....

Q2　An egg is dropped from the top of the Eiffel tower.
It hits the ground after 8 seconds, at a speed of 80 m/s.

　a)　Calculate the egg's acceleration. ....

　b)　How long did it take for the egg to reach a velocity of 40 m/s?

....

Q3　Ealing is about 12 km west of Marble Arch. It takes a tube train 20 minutes to get to Marble Arch from Ealing.

Only **one** of the following statements is true. Circle the appropriate letter.

　　A　The average speed of the train is 60 m/s.

　　B　The average velocity of the train is 10 m/s.

　　C　The average velocity of the train is 60 m/s due east.

　　D　The average speed of the train is 10 m/s.

　　E　The average velocity of the train is 10 m/s due west.

Q4　Paolo and some friends want to order a takeaway. Paolo writes down what they know about the two nearest takeaways:

Ludo's Pizza	Moonlight Indian Takeaway
• Time taken to cook the food is 1/4 hour	• Time taken to cook the food is 1/2 hour
• Distance to the house is 6.5 km	• Distance to the house is 4 km
• Deliver on scooters with average speed of 30 km/h	• Delivery van has average speed of 40 km/h

Remember to add on the time taken to cook the food.

Which takeaway should they order from to get their food the **quickest**?

....

Q5　A car accelerates at 2 m/s². After 4 seconds it reaches a speed of 24 m/s.

How fast was it going before it started to accelerate?

....

....

D-T and V-T Graphs

Q1 Steve walked to football training only to find that he'd left his boots at home. He turned round and walked back home, where he spent 30 seconds looking for them. To make it to training on time he had to run back at twice his walking speed.

Below is an incomplete **distance-time graph** for Steve's journey.

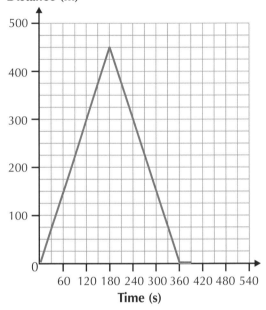

Distance (m)

a) How long did it take Steve to walk to training?

....

b) Calculate Steve's speed (in m/s) as he walked to training.

....

....

c) Complete the graph to show Steve's run back from his house to training (with his boots).

Q2 The distance-time graph and the velocity-time graph below both indicate the **same** three journeys.

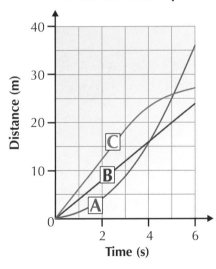

Distance-Time Graph

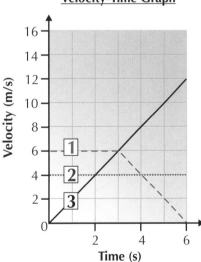

Velocity-Time Graph

Draw lines to show how the distance-time and velocity-time graphs match up.

Line A		Line 1
Line B		Line 2
Line C		Line 3

Physics 2(i) — Forces and Motion

D-T and V-T Graphs

Q3 Below is a velocity-time graph for the descent of a lunar lander. It accelerates due to the pull of gravity from the Moon.

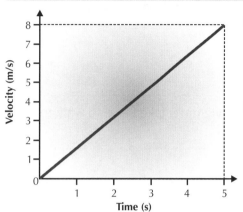

a) Use the graph to calculate the lander's acceleration.

....

b) Calculate the distance travelled by the lander during the five seconds of descent shown on the graph.

....

....

Q4 The speed limit for cars on motorways is 70 mph (about 31 m/s). A motorist was stopped by the police for speeding as she joined the motorway from a service station.

The distance-time graph on the right shows the car's acceleration. The motorist denied speeding. Was she telling the truth?

....

....

Q5 A motorist saw a kitten asleep on the road 25 m in front of him. It took him 0.75 seconds to react and slam on the brakes. The velocity-time graph below shows the car's deceleration.

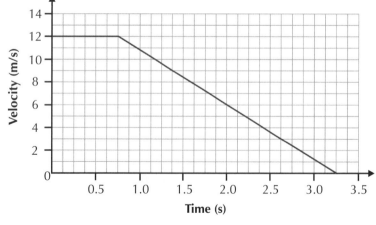

It helps to split the graph up into two smaller shapes.

Use the graph to work out whether the motorist stopped before hitting the kitten.

....

....

Physics 2(i) — Forces and Motion

Mass, Weight and Gravity

Q1 Which is the correct explanation for why the Moon orbits the Earth? Tick the appropriate box.

☐ There is an attractive force between the weights of the Earth and Moon.

☐ They attract each other as they have masses caused by them having weight.

☐ The weight of the Moon acts downwards.

☐ There is an attractive force between the masses of the Earth and Moon.

☐ The mass of the Moon acts downwards.

Q2 Two mad scientists are planning a trip to Mars.

a) Professor White tells Professor Brown —

"We won't need so much fuel for the return trip — the rocket will have less mass on Mars."

Is Professor White's reasoning correct? Explain your answer.

....

b) Professor Brown wants to investigate gravity on Mars. He takes to Mars a small fire extinguisher which weighs 50 N on Earth. He also takes his bathroom scales.

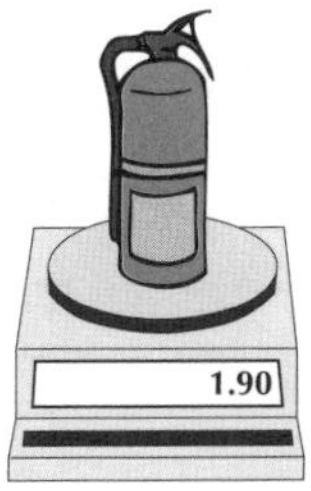

On Mars, Professor Brown weighs the fire extinguisher. The scales read **1.9 kg**. Calculate the **acceleration due to gravity** on Mars.

Find the mass of the fire extinguisher first.

1.90

....

....

....

Q3 A space probe lands on the icy surface of Europa, a moon of Jupiter. It weighs a set of known masses. The results are shown below.

Mass (kg)	0.1	0.2	0.3	0.4	0.5
Weight (N)	0.15	0.30	0.36	0.55	0.68

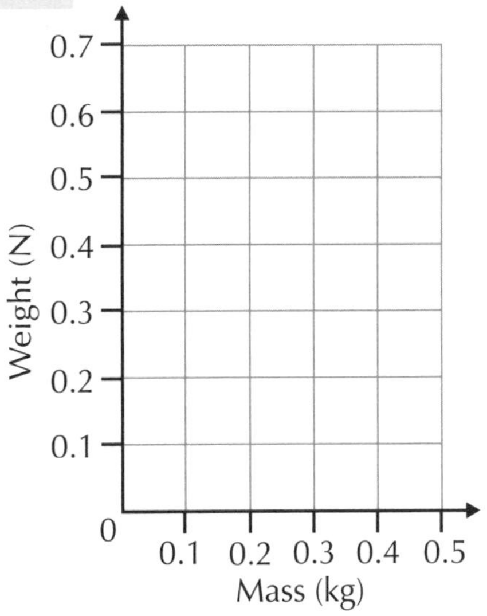

a) i) Plot a graph of this data on the axes given.

ii) Use your graph to estimate the gravitational field strength at Europa's surface.

....

....

b) Suggest why several masses were weighed, not just one.

....

The Three Laws of Motion

Q1   Use the words below to fill in the blanks.

proportional	force	reaction	stationary	accelerates	opposite
	constant	resultant	inversely	balanced	

Newton's 1st law: If the forces on an object are .... , it's either

.... or moving at .... speed.

Newton's 2nd law: If an object has a .... force acting on it, it

.... in the direction of the ....

The acceleration is .... to the force and

.... to the mass.

Newton's 3rd law: For every action there is an equal and ....

....

Q2   Otto is driving the school bus at a **steady speed** along a level road.
Tick the boxes next to any of the following statements which are **true**.

☐ The driving force of the engine is bigger than the friction and air resistance combined.

☐ The driving force of the engine is equal to the friction and air resistance combined.

☐ There are no forces acting on the bus.

☐ No force is required to keep the bus moving.

Q3   State whether the **forces** acting on these objects are **balanced** or **unbalanced**. Explain your answers.

a)   A **cricket ball** slowing down as it rolls along the outfield.

....

b)   A **car** going round a roundabout at a steady 30 mph.

....

c)   A **vase** knocked off a window ledge.

....

d)   A **satellite** orbiting over a fixed point on the Earth's surface.

....

e)   A **bag of rubbish** which was ejected from a spacecraft in empty space.

....

The Three Laws of Motion

Q4 The table below shows the **masses** and **maximum accelerations** of four different antique cars.

Car	Mass (kg)	Maximum acceleration (m/s^2)
Disraeli 9000	800	5
Palmerston 6i	1560	0.7
Heath TT	950	3
Asquith 380	790	2

Write down the names of the four cars in order of increasing driving force.

....

Q5 Jo and Brian have fitted both their scooters with the same engine. Brian's scooter has a mass of 110 kg and an acceleration of 2.80 m/s^2. Jo's scooter only manages an acceleration of 1.71 m/s^2.

a) What **force** can the engine exert?

....

b) Calculate the mass of Jo's scooter.

....

Q6 A spacecraft launches a probe at a constant speed. A day later, the probe returns at the same speed.

Did the probe have to burn any fuel? Explain your answer.

....

....

Q7 Maisie drags a **1 kg** mass along a table with a newton-meter so that it accelerates at **0.25 m/s^2**. The newton-meter reads **0.4 N**. Calculate the force of friction between the mass and the table.

....

....

Q8 Which of the following statements correctly explains what happens when you walk? Circle the appropriate letter.

  A Your feet push the ground backwards, so the ground pushes you forwards.

  B The force in your muscles overcomes the friction between your feet and the ground.

  C The ground's reaction can't push you backwards because of friction.

  D Your feet push forwards, and the ground's reaction is upwards.

The Three Laws of Motion

Q9 Which picture correctly shows the **weight** (w) and **reaction force** (R) for a car on a slope? Tick the appropriate box.

Q10 A camper van with a mass of 2500 kg has a maximum driving force of 2650 N.

  a) The camper van drives along a straight, level road at a constant speed of 90 kilometres per hour. At this speed, air resistance is 2000 N and the friction between the tyres and the road is 500 N.

    i) What force is the engine exerting? ....

    ii) Draw a diagram to show all the forces acting on the camper van.
Give the size of each force.

  b) A strong headwind begins blowing, with a force of **200 N**. The van slows down.
Calculate its deceleration.

    ....

  c) The driver notices that the van is slowing and puts his foot right down on the accelerator, applying the maximum driving force.

    i) Draw a diagram to illustrate the horizontal forces acting on the camper van now.

    ii) Work out how the velocity of the camper van changes when the driver puts his foot down. (Assume that air resistance and friction remain at their previous values.)

    ....

    ....

> **_Top Tips:_** A resultant force means your object will accelerate — it will change its speed or direction (or both). But if your object has a constant speed (which could be zero) and a constant direction, you can say with utter confidence that there ain't no resultant force. Be careful though — a zero resultant force doesn't mean there are **no** forces, just that they all balance each other out.

Drag and Terminal Velocity

Q1 Use the words supplied to fill in the blanks in the paragraph below about a skydiver.

decelerates   decrease   less   balances   increase   constant   greater   accelerates

When a skydiver jumps out of a plane, his weight is .... than his air

resistance, so he .... downwards. This causes his air resistance to

.... until it .... his weight. At this point, his

velocity is .... When his parachute opens, his air resistance is

.... than his weight, so he .... This causes his air

resistance to .... until it .... his weight. Then his

velocity is .... once again.

Q2 Which of the following will **reduce** the drag force on an aeroplane?
Tick any appropriate boxes.

☐ flying higher (where the air is thinner)   ☐ carrying less cargo

☐ flying more slowly   ☐ making the plane more streamlined

Q3 A scientist plans to investigate gravity by dropping a hammer and a feather from a tall building.
Three onlookers predict what will happen. Say whether each is right or wrong, and explain why.

Paola: "They will land at the same time — gravity is the same for both."

Guiseppe: "The feather will reach its terminal velocity before the hammer."

Raphael: "The hammer will land first — it has less drag compared to its weight than the feather does."

a) Paola is **right / wrong** because ....

....

b) Guiseppe is **right / wrong** because ....

....

c) Raphael is **right / wrong** because ....

....

Q4 Mavis is investigating **drag** by dropping balls into a measuring cylinder
full of oil and timing how long they take to reach the bottom.
She does the experiment with a **golf ball**, a **glass marble** and a **ball bearing**.

From this experiment, can Mavis draw any conclusions about
the effect of size on drag? Explain your answer.

....

....

Drag and Terminal Velocity

Q5 The graph shows how the velocity of a skydiver changes before and after he opens his parachute.

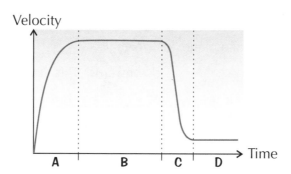

For each of the four regions A-D say whether the force of **weight** or **air resistance** is greater, or if they are **equal**.

	weight is greater	air resistance is greater	both equal
Region A:	☐	☐	☐
Region B:	☐	☐	☐
Region C:	☐	☐	☐
Region D:	☐	☐	☐

Q6 Two skydivers jump out of a plane. Kate opens her parachute after three seconds, when she is still accelerating rapidly. Alison doesn't open her parachute yet but uses her video camera to film Kate's skydive. On the film Kate's parachute appears to pull her suddenly upwards when it opens.

a) Is Kate really moving upwards? Explain your answer. ....

....

b) Describe how Kate's velocity changes when her parachute opens. ....

....

Q7 On **Venus**, atmospheric pressure is about 90 times that on Earth, but the gravitational field strength is about the same.
On **Mars**, atmospheric pressure is about 1/100th of that on Earth and the gravitational field strength is less than half that on Earth.

Higher atmospheric pressure means the atmosphere is thicker and provides more resistance.

Probes which land on other planets often need parachutes to slow them down during their descent. What **size** of parachute would you recommend, relative to a parachute used on Earth, for:

a) landing on Venus: ....

b) landing on Mars: ....

> **Top Tips:** When objects move through the air at high speed, the air resistance is proportional to the object's **velocity squared**. That's why, for skydivers, air resistance soon balances their weight and they reach terminal velocity. It's also why **driving** very fast is very **inefficient**.

Stopping Distances

Q1 **Stopping distance** and **braking distance** are not the same thing.

  a) What is meant by 'braking distance'?

    ....

  b) Use the words in the box to complete the following word equations.

braking	speed	reaction time	thinking

    i) Thinking distance = ... × ....

    ii) Stopping distance = ... distance + ... distance.

Q2 Will the following factors affect **thinking** distance, **braking** distance or **both**?
Write them in the relevant columns of the table.

tiredness   road surface   weather   speed

alcohol   tyres   brakes   load

Thinking Distance	Braking Distance

Q3 A car joins a motorway and changes speed from 30 mph to 60 mph.
Which one of the following statements is **true**? Tick the appropriate box.

☐ The total stopping distance will double.

☐ The braking distance will double.

☐ Thinking distance will double and braking distance will more than double.

☐ Both thinking and braking distance will more than double.

Q4 A car has just driven through a deep puddle, making the brakes wet.
Explain why this will increase the stopping distance of the car.

....

....

Physics 2(i) — Forces and Motion

Work Done

Q1   Circle the correct words to make the following sentences true.

a)   Work involves the transfer of **force** / **heat** / **energy**.

b)   To do work a **force** / **push** acts over a **distance** / **time**.

c)   Work is measured in **watts** / **joules**.

Q2   Indicate whether the following statements are **true** or **false**.

                                                      True False

a)   Work is done when a toy car is pushed along the ground. ☐ ☐

b)   No work is done if a force is applied to an object which does not move. ☐ ☐

c)   Gravity does work on an apple that is not moving. ☐ ☐

d)   Gravity does work on an apple that falls out of a tree. ☐ ☐

Q3   An elephant exerts a constant force of **1200 N** to push a donkey along a track at a steady 1 m/s.

a)   Calculate the work done by the elephant if the donkey moves **8 m**.

....

b)   From where does the elephant get the energy to do this work? ....

c)   Into what form(s) is this energy transferred when work is done on the donkey?

....

Q4   Ben's mass is 60 kg. He climbs a ladder. The rungs of the ladder are 20 cm apart.

a)   What force(s) is Ben doing work **against** as he climbs?

....

b)   As he climbs, what happens to the **energy** supplied by Ben's muscles?

....

....

                  20 cm

c)   How much work does Ben do when he climbs **10 rungs**? (Ignore any 'wasted' energy.)
Assume that g = 10 N/kg.

....

....

d)   How many rungs of the ladder must Ben climb before he has done **15 kJ** of work?
(Ignore any 'wasted' energy.) Assume that g = 10 N/kg.

....

....

Work Done

Q5 Two identical barrels, each weighing 800 N, need to be loaded onto a lorry. Fred lifts one barrel a distance of 1.5 m onto the lorry. Joe rolls the other barrel up a 4 m plank by exerting a constant force of 350 N. Who has done more work?

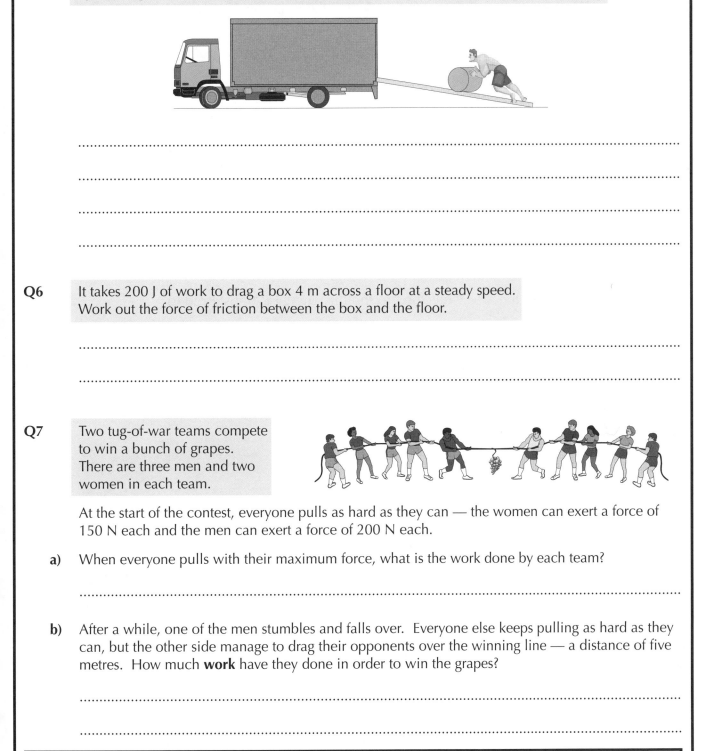

....

....

....

....

Q6 It takes 200 J of work to drag a box 4 m across a floor at a steady speed. Work out the force of friction between the box and the floor.

....

....

Q7 Two tug-of-war teams compete to win a bunch of grapes. There are three men and two women in each team.

At the start of the contest, everyone pulls as hard as they can — the women can exert a force of 150 N each and the men can exert a force of 200 N each.

a) When everyone pulls with their maximum force, what is the work done by each team?

....

b) After a while, one of the men stumbles and falls over. Everyone else keeps pulling as hard as they can, but the other side manage to drag their opponents over the winning line — a distance of five metres. How much **work** have they done in order to win the grapes?

....

....

Top Tips: Work is done when a force makes things **move**. E.g. an Arctic explorer pulling a sled over the ice exerts a **force** on the sled which makes it **move** a certain **distance**. To get the sled moving (from stationary), chemical energy from the explorer's food is transferred into kinetic energy (of the moving sled) and into heat (because of friction between the sled and the ice and in making the explorer a bit hot). Once the sled is moving at a steady speed, energy is still being transferred — enough to keep on overcoming friction (and to keep our brave hero all hot and sweaty).

Kinetic and Potential Energy

Q1 Robin Hood fires an arrow to signal to his band of merry men. He draws back the bowstring and releases the arrow, which flies into the air then falls back down again.

Complete the following passage which describes the main energy changes involved.

When the bowstring is drawn back, it stores ....

.... energy. This is transferred to

.... energy as the arrow is released and flies into

the air. As the arrow rises, it gains ....

.... energy and loses ....

energy. As the arrow falls, it gains .... energy

and loses .... energy.

When the arrow hits the ground this energy is transferred to

.... energy.

Q2 Find the **kinetic energy** of a 200 kg tiger running at a speed of 9 m/s.

....

....

Q3 A golf ball is hit and given 9 J of kinetic energy. The ball's velocity is 20 m/s. What is its **mass**?

....

....

....

Q4 A 60 kg skydiver jumps out of an aeroplane and free-falls. Find the skydiver's **speed** if she has 90 750 J of kinetic energy.

....

....

....

Kinetic and Potential Energy

Q5 Rachel pulls back a 0.002 kg rubber band and flicks it across a room with a speed of 10 m/s. What was the **elastic potential energy** stored in the rubber band just before it was released?

....

....

....

Q6 A 4 g bullet is fired from a rifle with a kinetic energy of 2 kJ. What is the **speed** of the bullet when it leaves the rifle?

....

....

....

Q7 The **braking distance** for a car travelling at **30 mph** is approximately **14 m**. At **50 mph** the braking distance is about **38 m**.

Explain, in terms of kinetic energy, why the braking distance more than doubles when the car's speed is less than doubled.

....

....

Q8 A skier with a mass of 70 kg rides a chairlift to a point 20 m higher up a ski slope. She then skis back down to the bottom of the chairlift.

a) Calculate the **work done** against gravity by the chairlift in carrying the skier up the slope. (Assume that g = 10 N/kg.)

....

....

....

....

b) Find the skier's **speed** when she reaches the bottom of the chairlift. Ignore the effects of friction and air resistance and assume that g = 10 N/kg.

....

....

....

Momentum and Collisions

Q1 Circle the correct words or phrases to make the following statements true.

a) If the velocity of a moving object doubles, its **kinetic energy** / momentum will double.

b) If you drop a suitcase out of a moving car, the car's momentum will **decrease** / increase.

c) When two objects collide the total momentum changes / **stays the same**.

d) When a force acts on an object its momentum **changes** / stays the same.

Q2 Place the following four trucks in order of increasing momentum.

Truck A
speed = 30 m/s
mass = 3000 kg

Truck B
speed = 10 m/s
mass = 4500 kg

Truck C
speed = 20 m/s
mass = 4000 kg

Truck D
speed = 15 m/s
mass = 3500 kg

....

....

....

(lowest momentum)   .... , ... , ... , ...   (highest momentum)

Q3 Shopping trolley A has a mass of 10 kg and is moving east at 4 m/s. It collides with trolley B which has a mass of 30 kg and is moving west at 1 m/s. The two trolleys join together.

a) Complete the diagram showing the masses and velocities of the trolleys **before** they collide.

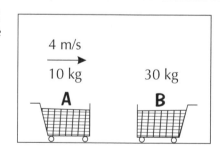

For this one you'll need to know the total momentum of the two trolleys before the collision.

b) Find the **velocity** of the trolleys **after** the collision (when they are joined) and draw a diagram showing their speed and direction.

....

....

....

....

Physics 2(i) — Forces and Motion

Momentum and Collisions

Q4 A 750 kg car is travelling at 30 m/s along the motorway. It crashes into the barrier of the central reservation and is stopped in a period of 1.2 seconds.

a) Find the size of the **average force** acting on the car to stop it.

....

....

b) Explain why the occupants of the car are likely to be less severely injured if they are wearing seatbelts made of slightly **stretchy** material.

....

....

Q5 A skateboarder with a mass of 60 kg is moving at 5 m/s. He skates past his bag, picks it up from the floor and slows down to 4.8 m/s. Find the mass of the skater's bag.

You might find it helpful to draw a diagram showing the masses and velocities involved.

....

....

....

....

Q6 A 0.15 kg cricket ball is dropped vertically onto a floor. It hits the floor at a speed of 10 m/s and bounces vertically back up at the same speed. If the ball is in contact with the floor for 0.02 s, what is the average force exerted on it?

How does the ball's velocity change?

....

....

....

....

Q7 A rocket is stationary in empty space. It is then propelled forwards by quickly releasing exhaust gases in the opposite direction. Indicate which of the following statements are **true**.

☐ The velocity of the exhaust gas is equal and opposite to the rocket's velocity.

☐ The momentum of the exhaust gas is equal and opposite to the rocket's momentum.

☐ The velocity of the exhaust gas is greater than the rocket's velocity.

☐ The momentum of the exhaust gas is greater than the rocket's momentum.

Mixed Questions — Physics 2(i)

Q1　Scott water-skis over a 100 m course. A forcemeter on the tow rope registers a force of 475 N.

a)　Calculate the **energy** needed to pull Scott over the course.

....

b)　The graph below shows how Scott's velocity changed over the course.
Describe his **acceleration**:

i)　between 0 and 5 seconds.

....

ii)　between 5 and 22 seconds.

....

iii)　after 30 seconds.

....

speed (m/s) vs *time (s)* graph

c)　Scott's mass is 75 kg. Find his kinetic energy 20 seconds after he started water-skiing.

....

....

d)　How far did Scott travel in the first 20 seconds?

....

....

Q2　Paul sets off from a junction on his scooter which produces a thrust of 270 N.
The total mass of Paul and his scooter is 180 kg.

a)　Calculate the initial acceleration of Paul's scooter.

....

b)　Calculate the size of the force produced when Paul applies his brakes and decelerates at 5 m/s^2.

....

c)　State two factors that would affect Paul's braking distance.

1. ....　　2. ....

d)　Explain why the total stopping distance would be increased if Paul were tired.

....

....

Mixed Questions — Physics 2(i)

Q3 During the production of a new film, a dummy is dropped 60 m from the top of a building. The dummy's weight is 950 N. Assume that $g = 10$ m/s^2.

a) Calculate the mass of the dummy.

....

b) How much gravitational potential energy does the dummy have before it is dropped?

....

....

c) How much kinetic energy will the dummy have when it reaches the ground?
(Ignore the effect of air resistance.)

....

....

d) Calculate the dummy's speed as it hits the ground.

....

....

e) An identical dummy wearing a parachute is dropped from the top.
Explain why this dummy will reach the ground travelling more slowly.

....

....

Q4 At the start of a race a motorcyclist accelerates to a speed of 90 km per hour in 5 seconds and then rides three laps at that speed. The total mass of the motorbike and rider is 200 kg.

a) Calculate the force needed to accelerate the motorbike during the first five seconds of the race.

....

b) A competitor on a better bike rides the same three laps at 135 km/h. Which bike would you expect to have consumed **more fuel** during the three laps? Explain your answer.

....

....

c) Explain why the motorbikes' tyres are likely to leave black skid marks on the track if the riders brake suddenly.

....

....

Mixed Questions — Physics 2(i)

Q5   The diagram shows Karl jumping between two stationary boats.

a)   When Karl leaps to the east from boat A, boat A moves west.
Explain why, using Newton's third law of motion.

....

....

b)   Karl has a mass of 80 kg and jumps with a velocity of 3 m/s east.
Boat A has a mass of 100 kg. What is its velocity just after Karl jumps?

....

....

....

c)   Boat B has a mass of 112 kg. Calculate boat B's velocity just after Karl lands in it.

....

....

....

d)   The distance travelled by boat B is plotted on the following graph.

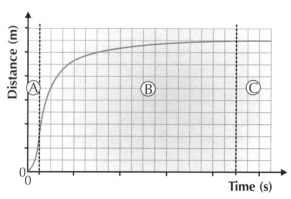

Describe what is happening to boat B's velocity during the periods A, B and C
shown on the graph.

i) A ....

ii) B ....

iii) C ....

Static Electricity

Q1   Fill in the gaps in these sentences with the words below.

electrons	positive	static	friction	insulating	negative

.... electricity can build up when two .... materials

are rubbed together. The .... move .... from one

material onto the other. This leaves a .... charge on one of the

materials and a .... charge on the other.

Q2   **Circle** the pairs of charges that would attract each other and **underline** those that would repel.

positive and positive   positive and negative   negative and positive   negative and negative

Q3   The sentences below are wrong. Write out a **correct** version for each.

a)   A polythene rod becomes negatively charged when rubbed with a duster because it loses electrons.

....

....

b)   A charged polythene rod will repel small pieces of paper if they are placed near it.

....

....

c)   The closer two charged objects are together, the less strongly they attract or repel.

....

....

d)   If a positively charged object is connected to earth by a metal strap, electrons flow through the strap from the object to the ground, and the object is safely discharged.

....

....

e)   Build-up of static can cause sparks if the distance between the object and the earth is big enough.

....

....

Static Electricity

Q4 A **Van de Graaff generator** is a machine which is used to generate static electricity. One type of Van de Graaff generator works like this:

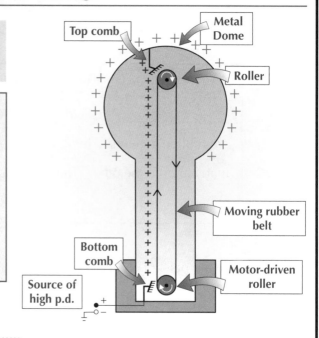

1. The bottom comb is positively charged and attracts electrons away from the rubber belt.

2. The rubber belt loses electrons and becomes positively charged.

3. As the positive charge on the belt passes the top comb, electrons are attracted from the metal dome onto the belt.

4. The dome loses electrons and builds up a positive charge.

a) Why is the belt made of rubber?

....

b) The top comb needs to be a **conductor**. Explain why.

....

....

c) Nadia is doing an experiment with a Van de Graaff generator. Her teacher tells her that if she touches the generator, she will become charged. When Nadia touches the generator, her hair starts to stand on end.

Use your knowledge of electrostatic charges to **explain why** Nadia's hair stands on end.

....

....

Q5 As Peter switched off his TV, he noticed that the screen was dusty. When he wiped it with his finger he heard a **crackling** sound and felt a slight **electric shock**.

Peter made two statements about what happened. Give a **reason** why he said each of the following:

a) *"The screen must have been at a high voltage."*

....

....

b) *"When I touched it, part of the screen was discharged to earth."*

....

....

Static Electricity — Examples

Q1   Smoke precipitators and photocopiers both use static charges.

Are the following **positively** or **negatively** charged?

	Positive	Negative
a) Collection plates in a smoke precipitator.	☐	☐
b) Smoke particles in a smoke precipitator.	☐	☐
c) Charged black powder in a photocopier.	☐	☐
d) Paper in a photocopier.	☐	☐

Remember — opposites attract.

Q2   Use the words below to fill in the gaps.

fuel	grain chutes	paper rollers	sparks	explosion	metal

Static electricity can be dangerous when refuelling cars. If too much static builds up, there

might be .... which can set fire to the ....

This could lead to an .... To prevent this happening, the nozzle is

made of .... so the charge is conducted away. There are similar safety

problems with .... and ....

Q3   Match up these phrases to describe what happens in a **thunderstorm**.
Write out your complete sentences below in the correct order.

If the voltage gets big enough...

... the voltage gets higher and higher.

The bottoms of the clouds become negatively charged...

... and knock electrons off.

As the charge increases...

... there is a huge spark (a flash of lightning).

Raindrops and ice bump together...

... because they gain extra electrons.

1. ....

2. ....

3. ....

4. ....

Static Electricity — Examples

Q4　In a **photocopier**, the image plate is **positively** charged.

a)　Why do some parts of the image plate lose their charge?

....

....

b)　Explain why the black powder sticks to the image plate.

....

c)　Describe what would happen if the paper wasn't charged.

....

Q5　Three friends are talking about static electricity on their clothes.

Why do some of my clothes get charged up during the day?

Lisa

Do cotton clothes get charged as much as nylon clothes?

Why do I hear a crackling sound when I take off my shirt?

Sara

Tim

Answer their questions in the spaces below.

Lisa: ....

....

Sara: ....

....

Tim: ....

....

Top Tips:　Static electricity's responsible for many of life's little annoyances — bad hair days, and those little shocks you get from touching car doors and even stroking the cat. Still, it has its uses too — the main ones you need to know about are **smoke precipitators** and **photocopiers**.

Circuits — The Basics

Q1 Use the words in the box to fill in the gaps. Use each word once only.

more
voltage
resistance
less
current
force

a) The flow of electrons round a circuit is called the ....

b) .... is the .... that pushes the current round the circuit.

c) If you increase the voltage, ... current will flow.

d) If you increase the ...., ... current will flow.

Q2 Match up these items from a standard test circuit with the **correct description** and **symbol**.

ITEM	DESCRIPTION	SYMBOL
Cell	The item you're testing.	—(A)—
Variable Resistor	Provides the voltage.	symbol
Component	Used to alter the current.	—⊣⊢—
Voltmeter	Measures the current.	—(V)—
Ammeter	Measures the voltage.	— symbol —

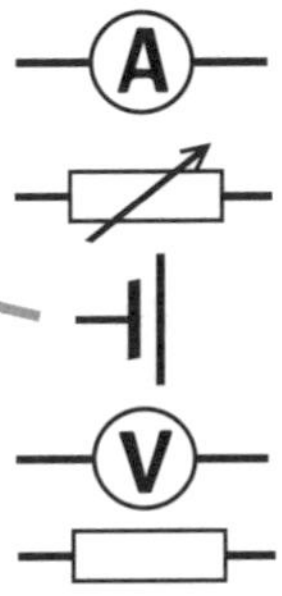

World's Strongest Current

Q3 Write down:

a) the **unit** of:

i) current ....   **ii)** voltage ....   **iii)** resistance ....

b) two ways of **decreasing** the current in a standard test circuit:

1. ....

2. ....

Q4 Indicate whether these statements are **true** or **false**.
Write out a **correct version** of the false statements.

	True	False
a) Current flows from positive to negative.	☐	☐
b) An ammeter should be connected in parallel with a component.	☐	☐
c) Items that are in series can be in any order.	☐	☐
d) A voltmeter should be connected in series with a component.	☐	☐

....

....

....

....

Physics 2(ii) — Electricity and the Atom

Resistance and V = I × R

Q1   Match the correct label to each of the **V-I graphs** below.

RESISTOR   FILAMENT LAMP   DIODE

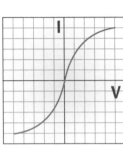   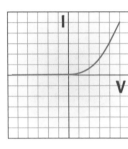   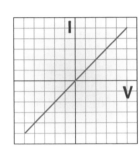

A ....   B ....   C ....

Q2   Indicate whether the following are **true** or **false**.
Write out a **correct version** of the false statements.

                                                                       True   False

a)   The resistance of a filament lamp decreases as it gets hot.   ☐ ☐

b)   The steeper the gradient of a V-I graph, the lower the resistance.   ☐ ☐

c)   Current can flow freely through a diode in both directions.   ☐ ☐

d)   The current through a resistor at constant temperature is proportional to the voltage.   ☐ ☐

e)   Current can flow both ways through a lamp.   ☐ ☐

....

....

....

....

Q3   The graph below shows V-I curves for four resistors.

$$\text{Gradient} = \frac{\text{vertical change}}{\text{horizontal change}}$$

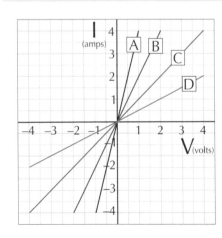

a)   Which resistor has the highest resistance?   ....

b)   Calculate the gradient of the line for resistor B.

....

c)   Calculate the resistance of resistor B.

....

Resistance and V = I × R

Q4 Fill in the missing values in the table below.

Use the formula triangle to help.

Voltage (V)	Current (A)	Resistance (Ω)
6	2	
8		2
	3	3
4	8	
2		4
	0.5	2

Q5 Peter tested **three components** using a standard test circuit. The table below shows his results.

Voltage (V)	−4.0	−3.0	−2.0	−1.0	0.0	1.0	2.0	3.0	4.0
Component **A** current (A)	−2.0	−1.5	−1.0	−0.5	0.0	0.5	1.0	1.5	2.0
Component **B** current (A)	0.0	0.0	0.0	0.0	0.0	0.2	1.0	2.0	4.5
Component **C** current (A)	−4.0	−3.5	−3.0	−2.0	0.0	2.0	3.0	3.5	4.0

a) Draw a **V-I graph** for each component on the axes below.

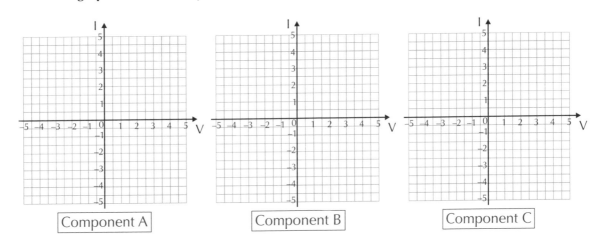

Component A   Component B   Component C

b) Complete Peter's **conclusions**:

Component **A** is a ....

Component **B** is a ....

Component **C** is a ....

Top Tips: There are two very important skills you need to master for resistance questions — **interpreting V-I graphs** and using the formula **V = I × R**. Make sure you can do both.

Circuit Symbols and Devices

Q1   Complete this table of devices and their circuit symbols.

Name of Device	Circuit Symbol
	⊶⋈⊷
thermistor	
switch open	
	⊦I
filament lamp	

Q2   Write out the names of the **numbered circuit devices** in the spaces below.

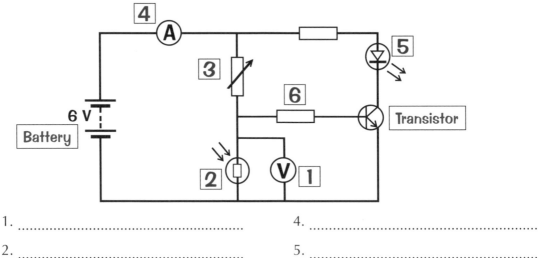

1. ....   4. ....

2. ....   5. ....

3. ....   6. ....

Q3   Use the words below to fill in the gaps.

light-dependent	diode	thermistor	fixed	variable	circuit

Some resistors always have the same resistance. These are called ....

resistors. A .... resistor can be used for altering the current in a circuit.

The resistance of a .... drops when the temperature increases.

The resistance of a .... resistor drops when light shines on it.

Circuit Symbols and Devices

Q4   Give one **similarity** and one **difference** between the following:

a)   a cell and a battery

....

....

....

b)   an ammeter and a voltmeter

....

....

c)   a thermistor and a light-dependent resistor.

....

....

Q5   Look at the components below.

a)   Use **some** of the above components to design a circuit that will vary the brightness of a **lamp**, depending on the **temperature** in the room.

b)   What happens to the **resistance** in the circuit as the room temperature **increases**?

....

c)   What happens to the **brightness** of the lamp as the room temperature **decreases**?

....

Top Tips: Circuit symbols aren't very exciting, so I'm not going to pretend otherwise.
You have to **learn** them though — or you won't have a clue what's going on with any of these questions.

Physics 2(ii) — Electricity and the Atom

Series Circuits

Q1   Match up these definitions with what they describe in a series circuit.

Same everywhere in the circuit

Shared by all the components

The sum of the resistances

Can be different for each component

Potential difference

Current

Total potential difference

Total resistance

Q2   Eva has drawn a series circuit she plans to set up, but she's made **three** mistakes.

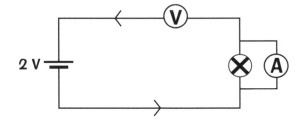

a)   List Eva's mistakes.

1. ....

2. ....

3. ....

b)   In the space below, **redraw** the circuit with the mistakes corrected.

Q3   The diagram shows a series circuit.

a)   Calculate the total potential difference across the battery.

....

2V 2V 2V

(A) 0.5 A

b)   Work out the total resistance.

....

R₁ R₂ R₃
2 Ω   4 Ω

c)   Calculate the resistance of resistor R₃.

....

For parts b) and d), you'll need to use the formula connecting V, I and R.

d)   What would you expect the reading on the voltmeter to be?

....

Physics 2(ii) — Electricity and the Atom

Series Circuits

Q4 Vikram does an experiment with different numbers of lamps in a series circuit. The diagram below shows his three circuits.

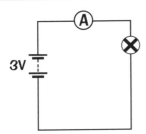 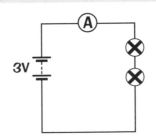 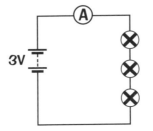 

a) What do you think happens to the **brightness** of the lamps as he adds more of them? **Explain** your answer.

....

....

b) How does the **current** change as more lamps are added? **Explain** your answer.

....

....

Q5 Here are some instructions for making a series circuit that will **vary the speed of a motor:**

> Connect the following in series...
>
> Two batteries — 3 V each
> Variable resistor
> Ammeter
> Motor of resistance 2 Ω (symbol (M))

a) Use the instructions to **draw** the circuit.

b) What happens to the **speed** of the motor as the resistance of the variable resistor is increased?

....

c) Calculate the **current** in the circuit when the resistance of the variable resistor is **1 Ω.**

....

....

Parallel Circuits

Q1 Tick to show whether these statements about parallel circuits are **true** or **false**.

True False

a) Components are connected side-by-side (instead of end-to-end). ☐ ☐

b) Each component has the same potential difference across it. ☐ ☐

c) The current is the same everywhere in the circuit. ☐ ☐

d) Components can be switched on and off independently. ☐ ☐

Q2 The diagrams show currents at junctions in two parallel circuits.

Write in the **missing** values.

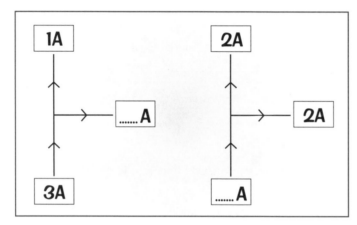

Q3 Find the **missing values** in this parallel circuit.

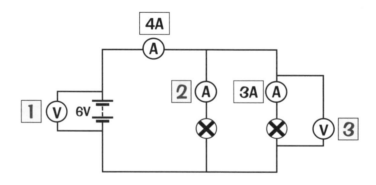

1. ....

2. ....

3. ....

__Parallel Circuits__

Q4   Karen does an experiment with different numbers of lamps
in a parallel circuit. The diagrams below show her three circuits.

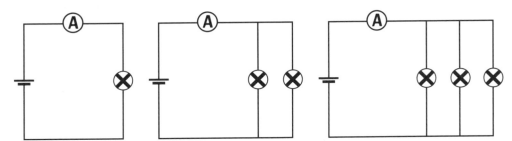

a)   What happens to the **brightness** of the lamps as Karen adds more of them? **Explain** your answer.

....

....

b)   What happens to the **ammeter** reading as more lamps are added? **Explain** your answer.

....

....

c)   One of the lamps in the third circuit is **unscrewed**.
What happens to the brightness of the other lamps?

....

Q5   Answer Shane's questions about parallel circuits.
Make sure you explain your answers.

a)   *"Can you have a different voltage and a different current in each branch of the circuit?"*

....

....

b)   *"Why do we use parallel circuits for the lights in our homes?"*

....

....

Series and Parallel Circuits — Examples

Q1   **Complete** this table for series and parallel circuits:

	SERIES CIRCUITS	PARALLEL CIRCUITS
Components connected	end to end	
Current		can be different in each branch
Voltage	shared between components	
Example of use		

Q2   A set of **Christmas tree lights** is designed to work on mains voltage (230 V). It has **12 V** bulbs.

  a)   How can you tell that these lights are wired in series?

    ....

    ....

  b)   Why might it be better to wire Christmas tree lights in **parallel**?

    ....

    ....

  c)   Give one reason why you can't usually swap bulbs between series and parallel sets of lights.

    ....

    ....

Q3   Fill in the **four** missing values on this **series** circuit:

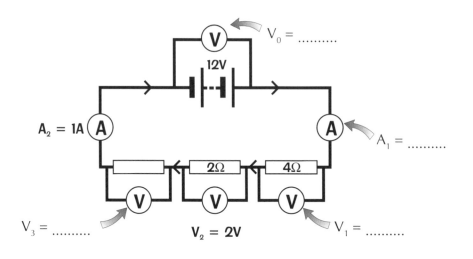

Series and Parallel Circuits — Examples

Q4 The diagram opposite shows a **parallel** circuit.

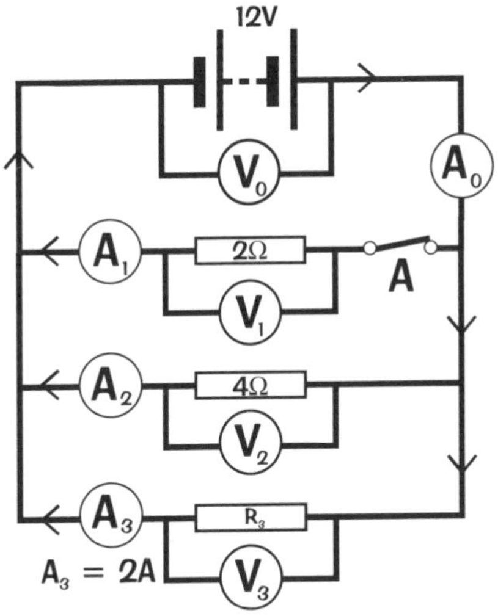

12V

V_0 A_0

A_1 2Ω   A
V_1

A_2 4Ω
V_2

A_3 R_3
$A_3 = 2A$ V_3

a) Calculate the readings on ammeters:

   i) A_1 ....

   ii) A_2 ....

b) Find the readings on voltmeters:

   i) V_1 ....

   ii) V_2 ....

c) What is the resistance of resistor R_3?

   ....

d) What is the reading on ammeter A_0 when switch A is open?

   ....

Q5 A group of pupils make the following **observations**:

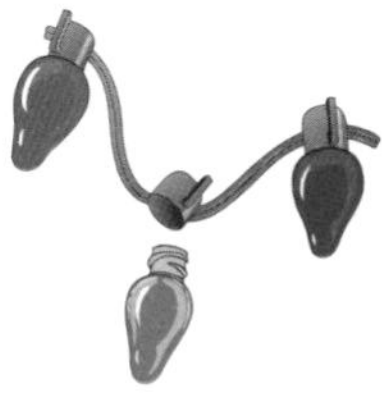

   1. *"The lights go dim if you switch the fan on in a parked car."*

   2. *"You can switch Christmas tree lights off by unscrewing one of the bulbs."*

   3. *"The lights in my house are wired in parallel, but all the wall lights in the living room go on and off together."*

Explain their observations.

1. ....

   ....

   ....

2. ....

   ....

   ....

   Think about what makes them go on and off.

3. ....

   ....

   ....

Top Tips: Now I know why my Dad used to spend ages fiddling around with the Christmas tree lights, trying to figure out which one didn't work. If only they'd been wired in parallel...
Make sure you understand all the **differences** between series and parallel circuits.

Mains Electricity

Q1   Choose from the words below to fill in the gaps.

changing	AC	hertz	DC	volts	direct
alternating	ohms	frequency	amps	direction	

> In the United Kingdom the mains electrical supply is about 230 ....
>
> The supply is .... current (..........) which means that the
>
> .... of the current is constantly ....
>
> The supply has a .... of 50 ....

Q2   Answer the following:

a)   What does "CRO" stand for?

....

b)   What does the trace on a CRO screen show?

....

c)   Give the names of the two main dials on the front of a CRO.

....

Q3   James connects a CRO to a power pack. By adjusting the power pack, he can alter the amount of voltage going across the CRO.

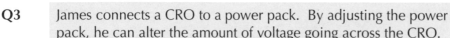

a)   Explain why the trace on the CRO screen is 'stretched' or 'squashed' vertically when James changes the voltage.

....

....

b)   Why is the trace 'stretched' or 'squashed' vertically when James moves the **gain** dial on the CRO?

....

....

c)   What happens to the trace when he moves the **timebase** control?

....

....

Mains Electricity

Q4   The diagram shows three traces on the same CRO. The settings are the same in each case.

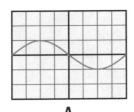   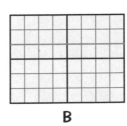   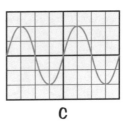

| A | B | C |

Write down the **letter** of the trace that shows:

a) the highest frequency AC ....,   **b)** direct current ....,   **c)** the lowest AC voltage ....

Q5   The diagram shows a trace on a CRO screen. The **timebase** is set to 10 ms per division, and the **gain** to 1 volt per division.

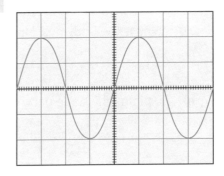

a)   What is the peak voltage? ....

b)   What is the time period?

....

c)   Calculate the frequency of the supply.

....

Q6   Jim is comparing two **computers** — one is designed for use in **Britain**, and the other in **America**. He looks at the manufacturers' badges, which give important information about the **electrical supplies** each computer needs.

BRITCOM — 884

Power supply	230 volts, 50 Hz
Fuse	3 A
Power consumption	20 W

This appliance must be earthed
British Computer Company, London

USCOM — 2800

Power supply	110 volts, 60 Hz
Fuse	3 A
Power consumption	25 W

Double Insulated
US Computers Inc., New York

Write down **two reasons** why the American computer would **not** be suitable for use in Britain.

1. ....

2. ....

Mains Electricity

Q7   Look at this picture of a kitchen. Put a **ring** round everything that is **unsafe**.

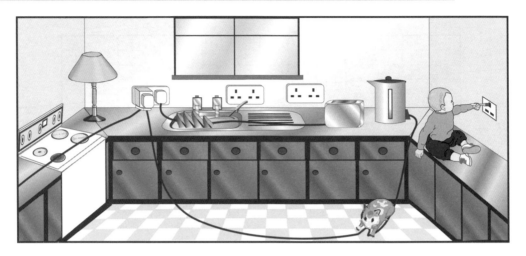

Q8   Answer the following questions about **plugs**:

a)   Why is the body of a plug made of rubber or plastic?

....

b)   Explain why some parts of a plug are made from copper or brass.

....

c)   What material is the cable insulation made from, and why?

....

Q9   Use the words below to complete these rules for wiring a plug.

outer   bare   live   earth   neutral   insulation   firmly   green and yellow

a)   Strip the .... off the end of each wire.

b)   Connect the brown wire to the .... terminal.

c)   Connect the blue wire to the .... terminal.

d)   Connect the .... wire to the .... terminal.

e)   Check all the wires are .... screwed in with no .... bits showing.

f)   The cable grip must be securely fastened over the .... covering of the cable.

Q10   This plug is **incorrectly** wired. Write down the **three** mistakes.

━━━ = Neutral
━━━ = Live
〰〰〰 = Earth

1.   ....

2.   ....

3.   ....

Fuses and Earthing

Q1 Put **ticks** in the table to show which wires match each description.

Description	Live	Neutral	Earth
Must always be connected			
Just for safety			
Electricity normally flows in and out of it			
Alternates between +ve and –ve voltage			

Morris thought it best to be earthed at all times — just in case.

Q2 **Match** up the beginnings and endings of these sentences:

The live and neutral wires...

A circuit breaker...

A Residual Current Circuit Breaker...

Any metal casing...

... should be connected to the earth wire.

... should normally carry the same current.

... does the same job as a fuse.

... can be used instead of a fuse and earth wire.

Q3 Answer the following questions about a **kettle**:

a) Suggest what could cause a surge of current in the kettle's circuit.

....

....

b) How would a fuse in the kettle's circuit help prevent electric shocks?

....

....

c) Molly chooses a fuse for the kettle. How should she decide what fuse to use?

....

....

Q4 These sentences describe how a **fuse** and **earth wire** work together to help prevent you getting an electric shock from your toaster. Put numbers in the boxes to show the order they should go in.

☐ The surge in current causes the fuse wire to heat up.

☐ Everything is now safe.

☐ A fault develops and the earthed casing becomes connected to the live supply.

☐ The live supply is cut off.

☐ The fuse blows.

☐ A large current now flows in through the live wire and out through the earth wire.

Energy and Power in Circuits

Q1 Indicate whether these statements are **true** or **false**.

		True	False
a)	An electric current almost always produces heat.	☐	☐
b)	Cells provide the electrical energy in most portable appliances.	☐	☐
c)	An appliance's fuse rating should be lower than its normal current.	☐	☐
d)	Components in a circuit can transfer electrical energy to other forms of energy.	☐	☐

Q2 Fill in the gaps using the words in the box. You might need to use some of the words more than once, or not at all.

power	current	lower	higher	how long	voltage

The total energy transferred by an appliance depends on .... it's used for

and it's .... The power of an appliance can be calculated using the

formula: power = ... × .... The fuse rating for an

appliance should be a little .... than its normal ....

Q3 Calculate the **amount** of electrical energy used by the following.
For each component, say what **forms** of energy the electrical energy is converted to.

a) A 100 watt lamp in 10 seconds: .... J.

Electrical energy is converted to .... and .... energy.

b) A 500 watt motor in 2 minutes: .... J.

Electrical energy is converted to ...., ... and .... energy.

c) A 1 kW heater in 20 seconds: .... J.

Electrical energy is converted to .... energy.

d) A 2 kW heater in 10 minutes: .... J.

Electrical energy is converted to .... energy.

Remember to put time in seconds and power in W.

Top Tips: Anything which supplies electricity is supplying **electrical energy**, which can be converted to other forms of energy — like heat or light. Remember that. And there are two **important formulas** for you to learn — one for energy and one for power.

Physics 2(ii) — Electricity and the Atom

Energy and Power in Circuits

Q4 Lucy is comparing **three lamps**. She connects each lamp in a circuit and measures the **current**. Her results are shown in the table below.

	Lamp A	Lamp B	Lamp C
Voltage (V)	12	3	230
Current (A)	2.5	4	0.1
Power (W)			
Energy used in one minute (J)			

a) Complete the table by filling in the missing values.

b) What rating of fuse would each lamp need? A = ..., B = ..., C = ...

Q5 An electric heater is rated at **230 V, 1500 W**.

a) Calculate the current it uses.

....

b) What rating of fuse should be used with this heater? Circle your choice.

   1 A   2 A   3 A   5 A   7 A   10 A   13 A

Q6 Sajid does an experiment to compare how much heat energy is lost by two resistors, A and B, when the same current flows in each. The instructions for his experiment have been mixed up.

a) Put numbers in the boxes to show the correct order for the instructions.

☐ Connect the resistor, put it into the water and take the temperature.

☐ Keep stirring the water until the temperature stops rising.

☐ Measure out exactly 100 ml of water and put it into a plastic beaker.

☐ Switch on the power for exactly 5 minutes.

☐ Take the temperature of the water again.

b) The water temperatures Sajid records are shown in the table below.

	Resistor A	Resistor B
Start temperature	7 °C	8 °C
End temperature	10 °C	15 °C

Which resistor, A or B, had the **higher** resistance? ....

Charge, Voltage and Energy Change

Q1   A 3 volt battery can supply a current of 5 amps for 20 minutes before it needs recharging.

  a)   Calculate:

   i) the number of seconds in 20 minutes.

   ....

   ii) how much charge the battery can provide before it needs recharging.

   ....

  b)   Each coulomb of charge from the battery can carry 3 J of energy.
       How much energy can the battery transform before it needs recharging?

   ....

Q2   Sally is comparing two lamps, A and B. She takes the measurements shown in the table.

	Lamp A	Lamp B
Current through lamp (A)	2	4
Voltage drop across lamp (V)	3	2
Charge passing in 10 s (C)		
Energy transformed in 10 s (J)		

   Calculate the **missing values** and write them in the table.

Q3   The motor in a fan is attached to a 9 V battery.
       If a current of 4 A flows through the motor for 7 minutes:

  a)   Calculate the total charge passed.

   ....

  b)   Calculate the energy transformed by the motor.

   ....

Q4   The following statements are wrong.
       Write out a correct version of each.

Look back at the formulas for charge and energy if you're puzzled.

  a)   Higher voltage means more coulombs of charge per second.

   ....

  b)   One ampere (amp) is the same as one coulomb per joule.

   ....

  c)   One volt is the same as one joule per ampere.

   ....

Atomic Structure

Q1   Number these different ideas about atoms in the order they were first thought of.

   A An atom is like a plum pudding, with electrons stuck into a ball of positive charge.
   B All materials are made of identical tiny particles called atoms.
   C An atom has a small nucleus with electrons whizzing around it.
   D Atoms contain electrons which can be removed from atoms.
   E Each element has its own kind of atom.

   Correct order: .... , ... , ... , ... , ...

Q2   Match up the key words with their meanings.

Keyword	**Meaning**
Isotopes	The part of an atom that has protons and neutrons.
Unstable atoms	Forms of an element which have different numbers of neutrons.
Nuclear decay	High-energy particles or waves that a decaying atom spits out.
Radiation	Atoms which are likely to break up (decay).
Nucleus	The random break-up of atomic nuclei

Q3 a)   **J J Thompson** showed that **John Dalton**'s theory of atomic structure wasn't quite right.

   i) Which part of John Dalton's theory was wrong?

   ....

   ii) What evidence did J J Thompson have to suggest that John Dalton's idea was wrong?

   ....

b) **i)** What was the new idea about atoms put forward by **Ernest Rutherford**?

   ....

   ii) What evidence led Rutherford to this new idea?

   ....

Q4   What are the important similarities and differences between:

   a) protons and neutrons

   ....

   ....

   b) protons and electrons

   ....

   ....

Radioactive Decay Processes

Q1 Complete the table showing the properties of the three types of radiation from radioactive decay.

	Alpha (α)	Beta (β)	Gamma (γ)
Ionising power		.	weak
Mass (a. m. u.)	4		
Penetrating power		moderate	
Speed			very fast
Charge	2+		

Q2 When a nucleus emits an alpha or beta particle, the nucleus changes.

a) What happens to a nucleus when it emits an **alpha particle**?

....

....

....

b) What happens to a nucleus when it emits a **beta particle**?

....

....

Q3 What is the connection between the ionising power of radiation and its penetrating power?

....

....

Q4 Explain clearly why:

Hint — think about the number of protons and neutrons.

a) an alpha particle is written as $^4_2$He or $^4_2\alpha$.

....

b) a radium atom $^{226}_{88}$Ra turns into a radon atom $^{222}_{86}$Rn when it emits an alpha particle.

....

c) a beta particle is written as $^0_{-1}$e or $^0_{-1}\beta$.

....

d) a carbon-14 atom $^{14}_6$C turns into a nitrogen atom $^{14}_7$N when it emits a beta particle.

....

Physics 2(ii) — Electricity and the Atom

Background Radiation

Q1 Tick any of the following statements that are **true**.

☐ Radon gas is given off by rocks such as granite.

☐ Exposure to radon gas increases the risk of getting lung cancer.

☐ Scientists are sure that radon gas is only dangerous at high levels of concentration.

☐ If you live where there is a lot of radon gas, there is nothing you can do about it.

☐ The risk from radon gas is the same whether you smoke or not.

Q2 List **five** sources of background radiation.

....

....

Q3 Peter did an experiment to compare equal quantities of two radioactive materials. Here are his results and conclusion.

Material tested	Radiation measured (counts per second)
None	50
Material A	200
Material B	400

CONCLUSION
"Both materials are radioactive. Material B is twice as radioactive as Material A."

a) Is Peter's conclusion correct? Give a reason for your answer.

....

....

b) What other conclusion could Peter have drawn?

....

Q4 Radon gas building up in people's houses is a problem.

a) Explain why it's a problem.

....

b) Why is the level of radon gas in homes different in different parts of the country?

....

....

c) What can be done to reduce the problem caused by radon gas in homes?

....

....

100

Nuclear Fission and Fusion

Q1 Match up each key word or phrase with its meaning.

Keyword	Meaning
Fission	A process which changes atomic nuclei.
Nuclear reaction	Joining together.
Fusion	A device using an uncontrolled nuclear reaction.
Atomic bomb	Splitting apart.
Nuclear reactor	A device using nuclear fusion.
Hydrogen bomb	A device using a controlled nuclear reaction.

Pu

n

Q2 Explain how a nuclear fission **chain reaction** occurs, starting with a single **plutonium** nucleus absorbing a **slow-moving neutron**.

....

....

....

....

Q3 List four differences between nuclear **fission** and nuclear **fusion**.

1. ....

2. ....

3. ....

4. ....

Q4 Give two good points and two bad points about **fusion reactors**.

Good points ....

....

Bad points ....

....

Top Tips: Nuclear fuel can provide **millions** of times more energy than the same mass of fossil fuel. Given the current concerns about CO_2 emissions from burning fossil fuels, you can see why many people see nuclear fuel as an attractive alternative. Nuclear waste is really **dangerous** though.

Mixed Questions — Physics 2(ii)

Q1   The diagram shows part of an ink-jet printer. Each droplet of ink is given a positive charge as it leaves the nozzle. Plates A and B are also charged.

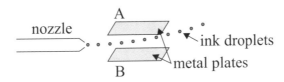

a)   What charges would plates A and B have to make the droplets bend upwards as shown?

....

b)   Explain how the droplets can be steered up or down to any desired position.

....

....

Q2   Maria walks across the nylon carpet in her living room and touches the radiator to see if the heating is on. When she touches the radiator, which is earthed, she feels an electric shock. Explain why.

....

....

Q3   Some railways use overhead electric cables at a voltage of 25 kV (25 000 V). Suggest why these cables must be kept a certain distance *d* away from bridges and other structures.

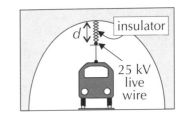

....

....

Q4   The diagram shows a circuit in which three resistors are connected in series.

a)   Calculate the total resistance of the 3 resistors.

....

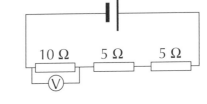

b)   If the voltmeter shown reads 4 V, find:

i)   the current flowing in the circuit. ....

ii)   the voltage of the power supply. ....

....

iii)   the energy dissipated in each of the 5 Ω resistors in 2 minutes.

....

....

Mixed Questions — Physics 2(ii)

Q5 The diagram shows a circuit which could be used for the lights on a car.
Each headlight bulb is rated at 12 V, 6 A and each side light bulb is rated at 12 V, 0.5 A.

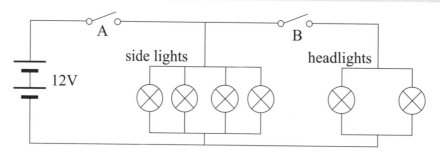

a) Calculate the total current flowing from the battery when:

i) Switch A is closed and switch B is open.

....

ii) Switch A is open and switch B is closed.

....

iii) Switches A and B are both closed.

....

b) A car's rear window de-mister is also connected to the battery in parallel.
Explain why the lights dim slightly when the de-mister is switched on.

....

....

c) A car battery supplies direct current (DC) but mains electricity is alternating current (AC).

i) The diagram shows a CRO trace from the mains
electricity supply on the island of Bezique.
The **timebase** dial was set to 10 ms per large division.

Calculate the **frequency** of Bezique's electricity supply.

....

....

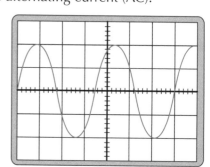

ii) On the diagram, illustrate
the CRO trace you would
see from a 12 V car battery
when the **gain** dial is set to
6 V per large division.

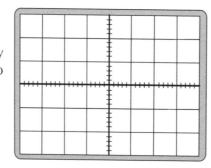

Mixed Questions — Physics 2(ii)

Q6 A 1.5 kW heater works off a 230 V mains electricity supply.

a) Calculate the **current** drawn by the heater. ....

b) What rating of **fuse** should be used in the heater's plug?
Circle your choice.　　1 A　　2 A　　3 A　　5 A　　13 A

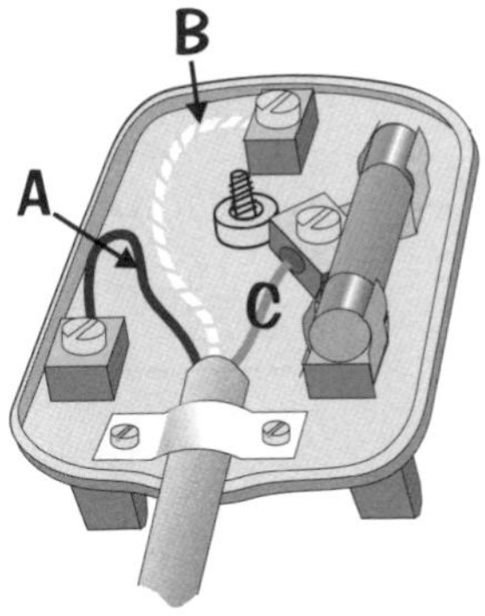

c) The diagram to the right shows a standard fused plug.

　i) Draw lines to match the appropriate letters to the names of the wires.

　　　　A　　　　B　　　　C

　　　　live　　　earth　　　neutral.

　ii) How does the 'earth' wire protect the user and the appliance from harm?

　　...

　　...

　iii) What types of appliances are safe to use without 'earthing'?

　　...

Q7 When radioactive decay occurs, α, β or γ radiation is emitted and new elements may be formed.

a) Write a nuclear equation to show thorium-234, $^{234}_{90}$Th, decaying to form protactinium, $^{234}_{91}$Pa .

....

b) **i)** Write a nuclear equation to show radon, $^{222}_{86}$Rn, decaying by **alpha** emission.

　　...

　ii) Radon gas makes up about 51% of the UK's background radiation. About 14% is from rocks
　　and building materials. How could **houses** be designed to minimise exposure to radiation?

　　...

　　...

Q8 The diagram shows the radioactive decay of an atom.

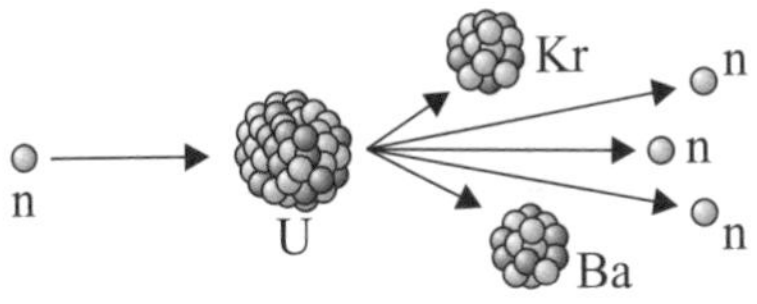

a) Underline the correct name for this type of radioactive decay.
　　　　fission　　　　　fusion

b) Describe how this process generates heat in nuclear reactors.

....

....

Turning Forces and Centre of Mass

Q1 a) Fill in the blanks in the following passage, using the words supplied.

pivot	perpendicular	moment	force

The turning effect of a .... is called its ....

It can be found by multiplying the force by the .... distance from

the line of action of the force to the ....

b) What are the units in which moments are measured? ....

Q2 To open a door, its handle needs to be **rotated clockwise**.

0.1 m

45 N

a) A force of 45 N is exerted vertically downwards on the door-handle at a distance of 0.1 m from the pivot. What is the **moment** of the force?

....

b) Pictures **A**, **B**, **C** and **D** show equal forces being exerted on the handle.

A   **B**   **C**   **D**

Which of the forces shown (**A**, **B**, **C** or **D**) exerts:

i) the largest moment? .... **ii)** the smallest moment? ....

Q3 A baby's pram toy consists of a toy banana hanging from a bar over the pram.

a) The banana is hanging **at rest**, as shown.
Draw a line on which the centre of mass **must** fall.

b) Complete the following sentences by choosing from the words and phrases below:

level with	vertically below	perpendicular	moment	centre of mass	horizontal

When a suspended object's .... is ....

the pivot, the .... distance between the line of action of the

gravitational force and the pivot is zero. This means that there is no

.... due to the object's weight.

Turning Forces and Centre of Mass

Q4 You can think of the **centre of mass** as the point where all the weight of an object acts.

a) Using lines of symmetry, find the centre of mass of each of these shapes:

b) **Circle** the correct answer to complete this sentence.
The centre of mass of a raindrop is:

A   at the top

B   near the top

C   midway down

D   near the bottom

E   at the bottom

Q5 Two men, one at each end, hold a 0.8 m long metal pole weighing 130 N so that it is in a **horizontal** position.
One man accidentally lets go of his end.

First, find the centre of mass of the pole.

What is the moment on the pole due to its weight an instant after he lets go?

Draw a diagram.

....

....

....

Q6 Some pupils want to find the centre of mass of an **irregularly shaped** piece of cardboard.
They are equipped with a stand to hang the card from, a plumb line and a pencil.
They make a hole near one edge of the card and hang it from the stand.

a) What steps should they take next in order to find the centre of mass?

....

....

....

....

b) How could they make their result more reliable?

....

....

Physics 3(i) — Forces and Waves

Balanced Moments and Stability

Q1   A 2 N weight (Weight A) sits 20 cm to the left of the pivot of a balance.
A 5 N weight (Weight B) is placed 16 cm to the left of the pivot.

a)   What is the moment exerted by **Weight A**? ....

b)   What is the moment exerted by **Weight B**? ....

c)   How far to the right of the pivot should Weight C (8 N) be placed to **balance** A and B?

....

d)   If all three of the weights were exactly **twice as far** away from the pivot,
would the balance tip over to one side? Explain your answer.

....

Q2   The top drawer of a two-drawer filing cabinet is full of heavy files, but the bottom drawer is empty.

Why is the cabinet in danger of falling over if the top drawer is fully pulled out?

....

....

Q3   The pictures show three different designs for **vases**.

Which vase will be **most stable**? Explain your answer.

....

....

Q4   One side of a drop-leaf table is pivoted on a hinge
and supported 5 cm from its edge by a table leg.
The table leaf is 80 cm long and weighs 40 N.

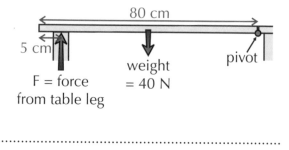

Find the force, F, exerted by the table leg (when the
table leaf is fully extended).

....

....

....

Circular Motion

Q1 Which of the following is the **best definition** of acceleration? Circle the appropriate letter.

A an increase in speed

B a change in direction

C an increase in velocity

D a change in velocity

E a change in speed

Q2 The diagram below shows a clock with hands that move **steadily** around the clock-face.

a) Draw and label with 'A' an arrow on the diagram to show the direction of the **velocity** of the tip of the **minute hand**.

b) Draw and label with 'B' an arrow to show the direction of the **acceleration** of the tip of the **hour hand**.

Q3 A **satellite** orbiting the Earth travels at a constant speed.

a) Is the satellite accelerating? Explain your answer.

....

b) Put a tick / ticks next the true statement or statements below.

☐ "If a body is accelerating then there must be a resultant force acting on it."

☐ "The forces acting on a body going round in a circle at a steady speed must be balanced."

☐ "If there is no resultant force acting on a body then it carries on moving in a straight line at the same speed."

c) What is the general name for a force that keeps a body moving in a circular path?

....

d) Draw lines to match up the following bodies with the force that keeps them moving in a circle.

A runner running round a circular track	Gravity
A satellite in orbit round the Earth	Tension
The seats at the ends of the spokes of a spinning fairground ride	Friction

Q4 Circle the correct options in these sentences.

a) The greater the mass of a body, the **smaller / greater** the force needed to keep it moving in a circle.

b) It takes a greater force to keep a body moving in a **smaller / larger** circle.

c) A cyclist rides round a circular track at a speed of 20 m/s. The frictional force between his tyres and the track is 1467 N. He speeds up to 21 m/s — the frictional force changes to **1617 N / 1331 N**.

Physics 3(i) — Forces and Waves

Gravity and Planetary Orbits

Q1   Fill in the blanks in the following sentences.

.... is the force that attracts one mass to another.   It provides the centripetal

force that keeps a planet in orbit around a .... All masses, even things like this

book, exert a gravitational attraction, but it is usually so .... we can ignore it.

Q2   The size of the gravitational force between two objects depends on their masses and how far apart they are.

a)   **Circle** the correct options in the following sentences:

For any two masses, the **greater** / **smaller** the two masses, the greater the force of gravity attracting them to each other.

For any two masses, the further they are apart, the **greater** / **smaller** the force of gravity attracting them to each other.

b)   At a particular time the planet Neptune and a comet are equally far away from the Sun. Which is attracted more strongly by the Sun's gravity? Why?

....

....

Q3   Each planet's orbits is a slightly different **shape** and the planets all move at different **speeds**.

a)   Describe the shape of the Earth's orbit around the Sun? ....

....

b)   Look at the sketch below of Mercury's orbit around the Sun. **Circle** the arrow, **A – E**, which shows the direction of the **force** exerted on Mercury by the Sun at that point in its orbit.

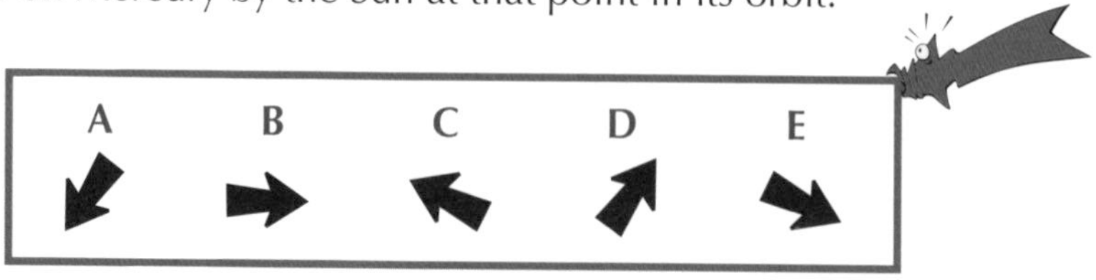

c)   Complete the following passage, choosing from the words in the box.

orbit	energy	galaxy	nearer	gravity	distance

A planet moving past a star has its path pulled into a curve by the star's

.... If the planet is moving at just the right speed its path will

come back on itself and form an .... To stay in orbit at a

particular .... , a planet must move at a particular speed.

d)   Which move **faster**, planets closer to the Sun or planets further away from the Sun?

....

Gravity and Planetary Orbits

Q4 The table below shows the **times** taken by several planets to complete their orbits. Some parts of the table have been left blank.

Planet	Approximate distance from Sun (million km)	Orbital period (Earth days)
Mercury	58	88
Venus	108	
Earth	150	
Mars	228	687
Jupiter		4331
Saturn	1434	10 747
Uranus	2873	30 589
Neptune	4496	
Pluto		90 588

a) Which planet is 779 million km from the Sun? ....

b) Which planet has an orbital period of 225 days? ....

Think about how many days Earth's orbital period has.

Q5 Satellites have lots of uses. **Different types** of satellite are needed for different applications.

a) Explain how a satellite in **low polar orbit** can scan the whole surface of the globe in a day.

....

....

b) Give one use of low polar orbiting satellites.

....

c) Tick **true** or **false** for each of these statements.

		True	False
i)	All geostationary satellites take the same time to make one orbit.	☐	☐
ii)	A geostationary orbit must pass above the equator.	☐	☐
iii)	A geostationary orbit must pass above the poles.	☐	☐
iv)	A geostationary satellite can orbit in any direction.	☐	☐

d) Explain why satellites which transmit TV and telephone signals are put into **geostationary** orbits.

....

e) Are artificial satellites outside the influence of Earth's gravity? How do you know?

....

Top Tips: Gravity's a busy force — it keeps us all stuck to the ground, it keeps the Moon orbiting the Earth, and still has time to keep all the planets spinning round the Sun. I'm impressed.

Images

Q1 Images formed by mirrors or lenses can either be **real** or **virtual**.

a) What is the difference between a real and a virtual image?

....

....

b) State whether the following images are real or virtual:

i) an image you see in a plane mirror. ....

ii) an image formed on the retina of your eye. ....

iii) an image you see when looking through a magnifying glass. ....

c) What **three** pieces of information do you need to give to describe the nature of an image?

....

Q2 The diagram shows a **pinhole camera**. Light from a goat passes through a pinhole to form an image on a tissue paper screen.

tissue paper

pinhole

image

goat

Draw rays from the top and bottom of the object showing how the image is formed.

Q3 Light can be both **reflected** and **refracted**.

a) In answer to a physics question, Harold writes: "I know that no reflection occurs when I look at a wall because if the wall reflected any light I'd see my reflection in it." Explain why he is wrong.

....

b) What is the relationship between the angle of incidence and the angle of reflection?

....

c) What does it mean when we say that a beam of light "refracts" when it enters a different medium?

....

d) What causes refraction? Circle one of these alternatives.

A Refraction is caused by an image being formed at the boundary between two media.

B Refraction is caused by light being reflected off the boundary between two media.

C Refraction is caused by one medium being better able to absorb light than another.

D Refraction is caused by light changing speed as it enters another medium.

Mirrors

Q1 The diagram below shows a pencil being reflected in a **plane mirror**. Some of the rays have already been drawn in.

a) On the diagram, draw in the rays showing how light is reflected to form an image of the **top** of the pencil.

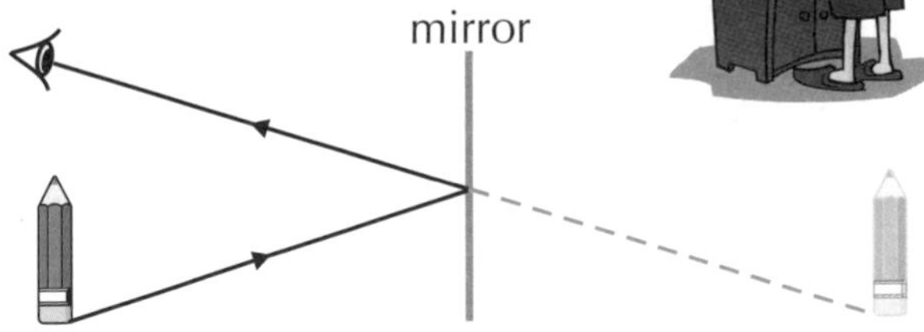

b) Is the image in a plane mirror real or virtual?

....

mirror

Q2 Below are four sentences about **curved** mirrors. Put them in the correct spaces in the table.

Reflective on outside of curve.   Reflected light converges.

Reflective on inside of curve.   Reflected light diverges.

	Description	Behaviour of parallel rays shining on mirror
Concave mirror		
Convex mirror		

Q3 The diagram below shows a curved mirror.

On the diagram, label the:

axis,

focal point,

vertex,

centre of curvature.

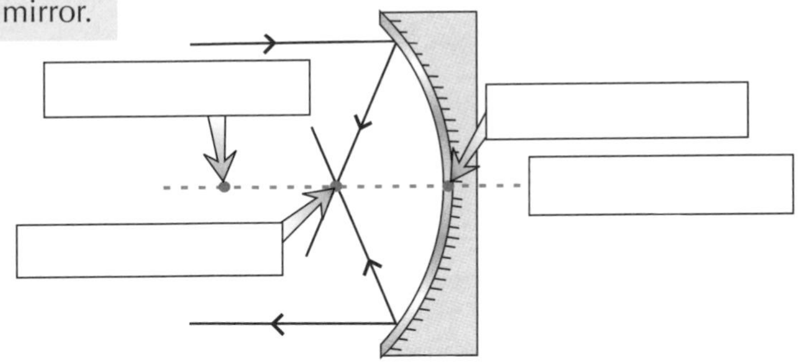

Q4 The diagram below shows an object in front of a uniform concave mirror. F is the focal point.

a) What happens to an incident ray that passes through the **focal point**?

....

....

....

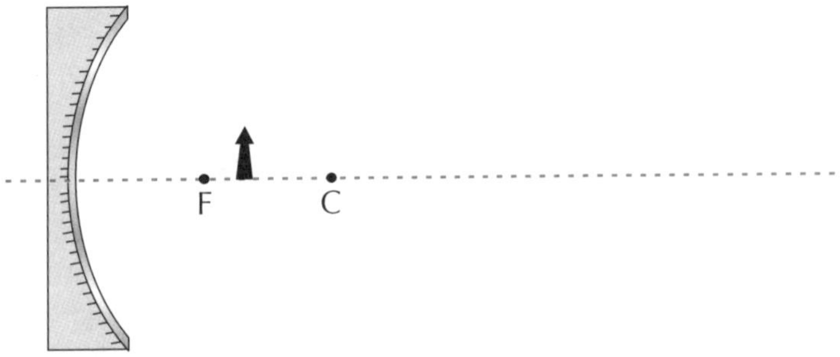

F   C

b) On the diagram, draw rays to construct an image of the object (the arrow shape).

c) The object is moved steadily along the axis, away from the mirror, until it reaches a point to the **right** of the **centre of curvature** (C) of the mirror.

i) Describe what happens to the **size** of the image as the object is moved past C.

....

ii) Describe what happens to the **position** of the image as the object is moved past C.

....

Physics 3(i) — Forces and Waves

Mirrors

Q5 Julie is holding a small concave mirror in front of her in order to do her lipstick. The focal length of the mirror is 3 m. Tick **true** or **false** for each statement.

True False

a) She sees a real image in the mirror.

b) The distance from the vertex to the centre of curvature is 6 m.

c) The mirror gives a magnified picture of her face.

d) The mirror gives a wider field of view than a plane mirror.

Q6 A car's **rear-view mirror** often has a **convex** shape.

a) State one other practical use for a convex mirror.

....

b) What property of convex mirrors makes them useful as rear-view mirrors?

....

Q7 An incident ray that is parallel to the axis will be reflected from a convex mirror so that the reflected ray **seems** to come from the focal point.

a) Explain why the reflected ray can't have actually come from the focal point.

....

b) In the sentence below, **circle** the correct words from the choices given.

An **extended** / **incident** ray that can be **extended** / **refracted** to pass through the focal point of a convex mirror will be reflected **along the normal** / **parallel to the axis**.

Q8 The diagram shows an object reflected in a convex mirror.

a) The diagram shows a ray from the top of the object striking the mirror. The dotted line shows the path the ray would have taken if the mirror wasn't there. On the diagram draw how the ray is reflected. Label the reflected ray as "Ray 1".

Hi

Ray 1

Hello

Ray 2

F

b) Draw the path of a ray coming from the top of the object parallel to the axis. Label the reflected ray as "Ray 2".

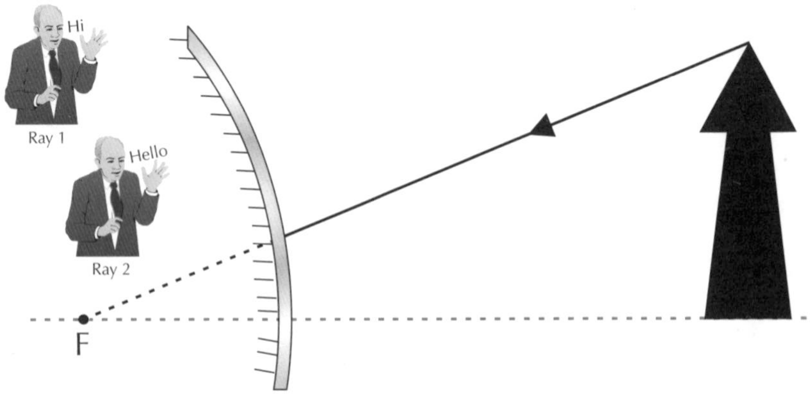

The top of the image is where Ray 1 and Ray 2 appear to come from.

c) Sketch the position of the image on the diagram.

Top Tips: When it comes to answering tricky questions, remember: the ray diagram is your friend. Don't panic — just draw in each ray carefully, one at a time, and Bob's your hamster.

Lenses

Q1 The diagram shows a ray of light passing across the **boundary** between two media.

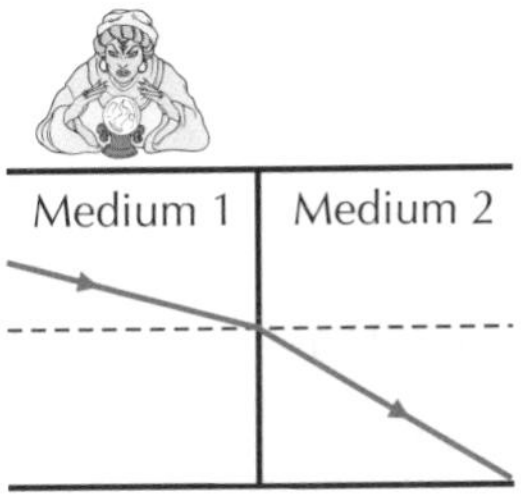

Medium 1 | Medium 2

a) Which of Medium 1 and Medium 2 is air and which is glass?

Medium 1 is .... Medium 2 is ....

b) Explain your answer to a). ....

....

Q2 Benedict shines a beam of light at an angle through three glass prisms.

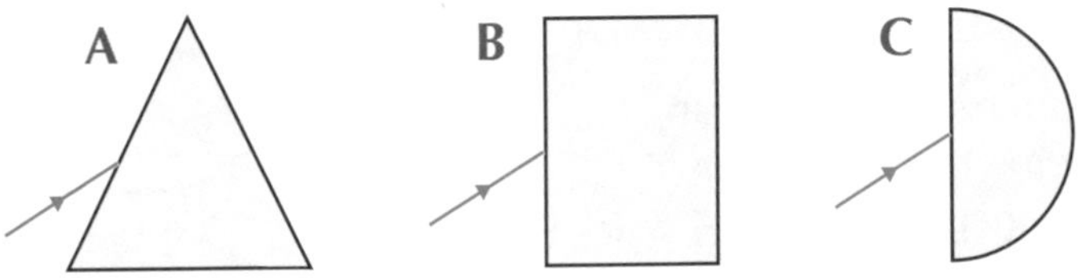

A   **B**   **C**

Sketch in the <u>normal</u> to each boundary first (Prism C's a bit tricky).

a) For each prism sketch the path the beam takes as it passes through and out the other side.

b) A beam of **white light** is sent into each of the prisms.
What would you see happening to the white light as it leaves Prism A?

....

c) What would you see as white light left Prism B? Explain your answer.

....

....

d) Which of these colours of light is refracted the **least**? **Circle** the correct answer.

violet   green   blue   red   orange

Q3 Lenses can be either **converging** or **diverging**.

a) Which type of lens has a virtual focus? ....

b) In the following sentences the words **parallel**, **converging**, **focal point** and **incident** have been replaced by the letters **W**, **X**, **Y**, **Z**. Write down which words are represented by **W**, **X**, **Y** and **Z**.

An **W** ray passing through the centre of a **X** lens from any angle carries on in the same direction.

A **X** lens causes all **W** rays **Y** to the axis to meet at the **Z**.

A **X** lens causes all **W** rays passing through the **Z** to emerge **Y** to the axis.

W .... **X** .... **Y** .... **Z** ....

c) Which of the following incident rays do not have their direction changed by either type of lens?
Tick any boxes which apply.

☐ Any ray parallel to the axis   ☐ Any ray passing through the centre of the lens

☐ Any ray passing along the axis   ☐ Any ray passing through the focal point

Lenses

Q4 In the ray diagrams below, the pictures of the lenses have been removed.

a) What type of lens could this be? Underline the correct answer from the options below.

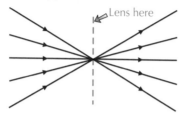

A A converging lens

B A diverging lens

C Neither a converging nor a diverging lens

D Either a converging or a diverging lens

b) On the diagram to the right, draw a lens of the correct type in the right position to complete the ray diagram.

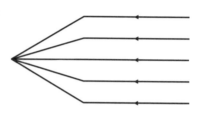

Q5 Some of this diagram has been hidden. Draw in the rest of the diagram, showing the position of the **object** that produced the image you see.

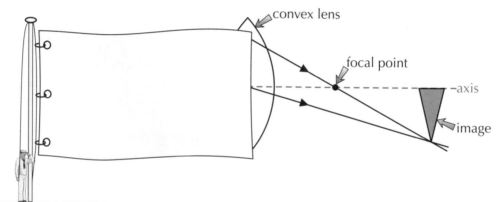

Q6 The table below gives information about the images formed by a **converging lens** when the object is at different positions, where F is the focal point of the lens.

Distance from lens to object	Distance from lens to image	Type of image	Size of image
Greater than 2F	Between 2F and F	Real, inverted	Smaller than object
Equal to 2F		Real, inverted	
Between 2F and F	Greater than 2F		
Less than F	Greater than 2F		Larger than object

a) Fill in the blanks in the table.

b) An object has a height of 1 cm. It stands on the axis of a converging lens, 5 cm away from it. The focal length of the lens (distance from the lens to the focal point) is 2.5 cm.

i) What size will the image be?

....

ii) Where will the image be formed, relative to the lens and the object?

....

Lenses

Q7   The diagram shows a **diverging lens**.

a)   Draw the path of a ray passing through the lens **along the axis** from left to right.

b)   Draw the paths of two incident rays **parallel** to the first ray, one **above** and one **below** the axis.

c)   Sketch in the position of the **virtual focal point** for the rays shown and label it "F".

Q8   An aubergine is placed 6.1 cm away from a converging lens with a focal length of **7 cm**.

a)   Will the image formed by the lens be:

   i)   upright or inverted? ....

   ii) on the same side of the lens or on the opposite side? ....

   iii) real or virtual? ....

b)   The aubergine is now placed at a distance X from the lens. The image is now bigger than the object and inverted. Which of the options below could be distance X? Circle your answer.

   A   3.9 cm   B   7.0 cm   C   10.2 cm   D   14.0 cm   E   15.3 cm

Q9   Circle the correct options in this description of images formed by **diverging lenses**.

Diverging lenses always produce **real / virtual**, **upright / inverted** images which are **smaller / larger** than the object.

Q10   The diagram below shows an object placed next to a diverging lens. The focal points are marked.

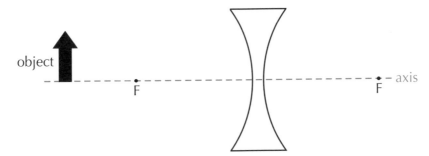

a)   On the diagram, draw the path of a ray coming from the top of the object and travelling in the direction of the centre of the lens.

b)   Draw the path of a ray coming from the top of the object and going towards the focal point on the far side of the lens.

c)   Draw the image formed by the lens.

Uses — Magnification and Cameras

Q1   Mr Richards is using a **magnifying glass** to read a magazine by the light of an overhead lamp.

a)   What sort of lens is used in a magnifying glass?

....

b)   Explain why an object you want to view with a magnifying glass must be placed nearer to the lens than the focal point.

....

c)   The writing on the magazine is in focus when the lens is a distance of 9 cm or less from the magazine. When the magnifying glass is held exactly 26 cm from the magazine a sharply focused image of the light bulb appears on the magazine.

Three of the following statements are **true**. Circle the appropriate letters.

> A   The lens works as a magnifying glass when it is held anywhere nearer than 26 cm to the magazine.
>
> B   The lens works as a magnifying glass when it is held anywhere nearer than 9 cm to the magazine.
>
> C   The focal length of the lens is 26 cm.
>
> D   The focal length of the lens is 9 cm.
>
> E   The image of the light bulb projected onto the magazine is a real image.
>
> F   The image of the light bulb projected onto the magazine is a virtual image.

Q2   The magnification of a magnifying glass depends on the distance of the object from the lens.

a)   State the formula for the magnification produced by a lens or mirror.

....

b)   A handwriting expert is studying a handwritten letter "A" with a magnifying glass. The letter is 0.5 cm high. When a magnifying glass is held 10 cm from the letter, the image of the letter appears to be 0.8 cm high. What is the magnification of the glass at that distance?

....

....

c)   The same magnifying glass is used to look at a ring made from a strip of gold of width 3 mm. The ring is also held 10 cm from the glass. How wide will the image be?

....

heh
heh
heh...

Physics 3(i) — Forces and Waves

Uses — Magnification and Cameras

Q3   A converging lens has a focal length of **8 cm**.
An object of height **3 cm** stands on the axis, **4 cm** away from the lens.

a)   Make a scale drawing to estimate to the nearest centimetre
the **height** of the image and how **far away** it is from the lens.

Height of image ....

Distance of image from lens ....

b)   What is the **magnification** of the lens at this distance?

....

Q4   Tuan is photographing a football match for his school magazine.

a)   How is the image produced in a camera similar to the image produced in a human eye?

....

b)   Explain why Tuan can't take a picture of an object closer than the focal length of the camera lens.

....

....

c)   Circle the correct words or phrases from the alternatives given in the following passage.

For the photograph not to be blurred the image must be formed **at the lens / between the lens and the film / on the film**. The image is formed at different **distances from the lens / magnifications** depending on how far away the object being photographed is. That is why the lens can be moved **back and forth / left and right**.

Top Tips: Digital cameras form images in more or less the same way as film cameras.
The only difference is that the image is projected onto a light-sensitive grid rather than a strip of film.

Physics 3(i) — Forces and Waves

Sound Waves

Q1   Sound waves are caused by **vibrations**.

Put the following sentences in the correct order to describe how the sound of a drumbeat is made and reaches our ears.

A   The vibration of the drum sets the air molecules next to it vibrating too.

B   We hear the sound when the vibrations in the air set our eardrums vibrating at the same frequency.

C   When someone beats a drum, the skin on top of the drum vibrates.

D   A series of compressions and decompressions travel outwards through the air (or other medium) as a longitudinal wave.

Correct order: .... , ... , ... , ...

Q2   This table shows the speed of sound in water, wood and air at room temperature.

Medium	Speed of sound (m/s)
wood	4120
water	1497
air	344

a)   In which of the three media does sound travel most slowly? ....

b)   Based on the data, does sound travel faster through a liquid or a solid? ....

Q3   Choose from the words below to fill in the spaces in the passage.

high   wavelength   amplitude   low   refract   frequency   quiet   vibrate

A sound wave makes air molecules .... If there are many vibrations

per second the frequency or pitch of the sound is .... If there are only

a few vibrations per second the pitch of the sound is .... If the air

molecules vibrate with a large .... the sound is loud. If each air

molecule vibrates over a small distance then the sound is ....

Q4   Most humans can hear sounds in the frequency range 20 Hz to 20 000 Hz.

a)   What is the frequency of a sound wave that has 30 compressions in one second?

....

b)   Put the following frequencies in order, from the lowest frequency to the highest.

3 MHz, 8 kHz, 630 Hz, 400 kHz, 5 Hz, 21 kHz

....

Sound Waves

Q5 Mina sings in her school choir. She practises both in her bedroom and in an empty practice room at school. She hears a difference in the sound of her voice, caused by a difference in echo.

a) What is an echo?

....

b) Why were there lots of echoes in the unfurnished practice room but not in her bedroom at home?

....

Q6 In an experiment, a ringing alarm clock is placed in a glass bell jar. Air is sucked out of the jar by a vacuum pump.

a) What happens to the sound and why?

....

....

b) Why does the experiment work better if the alarm clock is placed on top of a block of foam?

....

Q7 This CRO trace shows the waveform for a clear, pure note.

1 division = 0.005 s

a) What is this type of wave form called?

....

b) How long does one full vibration take?

....

1 Hz is one vibration per second.

c) What is the frequency of the wave in hertz?

....

d) On the same diagram, draw a waveform for a sound that has the same frequency but is louder.

Q8 Different types of instrument, e.g. a piano and a trumpet, will always sound different, even if they're producing notes of the same pitch and loudness.

How is the quality of a note shown on its oscilloscope trace?

....

Ultrasound

Q1 a) What is ultrasound?

....

b) How can ultrasound of a particular frequency be generated?

....

....

Q2 Yesterday Sean used an oscilloscope to study the frequency and amplitude of ordinary sound waves. Today he needs to use the same piece of equipment to study ultrasound.

What adjustment does he need to make to the oscilloscope?

....

Q3 Ultrasound can be used to detect the existence of a different medium below the surface of an object, and to measure how far below the surface it is.

Sketch a diagram showing what happens when an ultrasound wave hits the boundary between one medium and another.

Q4 Ultrasound can be used to clean delicate computer equipment.

a) State one advantage of using ultrasound to clean delicate computer equipment.

....

b) Choose from the following words to complete the blanks.

shaken	frequency	amplitude	vibrate	particles	heat

When an ultrasound beam is directed onto the equipment, both the equipment and the dirt attached to it start to .... at the .... of the ultrasound. The dirt is broken up into small .... and .... off.

Ultrasound

Q5   A building engineer suspects that there is a crack in a ceiling girder.
He uses an ultrasonic scanner to send a beam of ultrasound into the girder.

a)   If a crack is present, describe the two boundaries that the ultrasound wave will encounter.

....

....

b)   The diagram shows a beam of ultrasound striking the first of two boundaries.
Sketch what happens to the beam next.

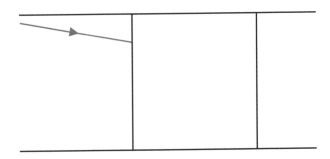

c)   Why is it important to know the speed of sound in a medium between two boundaries in order to discover how far apart the two boundaries are?

....

....

Q6   Bats "see" using ultrasound, so they have a lot in common with ultrasound scanners.

a)   Statements A, B and C describe three steps in making an ultrasound scan. Decide on the correct order for the statements and write the letters in the left-hand column of the table.

    A The internal computer processes data on the delays between pulses and echoes to produce an image on the monitor.

    B The scanner sends out pulses of ultrasound.

    C The scanner detects the reflected pulses via a microphone.

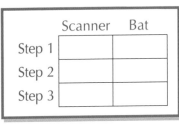

	Scanner	Bat
Step 1		
Step 2		
Step 3		

b)   Bats use ultrasound to help them find their prey. Decide on the correct order for statements D, E and F and write the letters in the right-hand column of the table.

    D The bat listens for echoes bounced off the bodies of insects.

    E The bat instinctively uses the time taken for the echo to locate its prey.

    F The bat emits an ultrasonic squeak.

Ultrasound

Q7   Ultrasound is used to make pre-natal scans of a fetus.

a)   For pre-natal scanning, why is it better to use ultrasound than X-rays?

....

....

b)   Use the key words below to write a brief explanation of how a pre-natal scan works.

reflected	monitor		fetus	uterus
boundary	image	processed	amniotic fluid	ultrasound

....

....

....

....

c)   Write down another medical use of ultrasound.

....

Q8   A pulse of ultrasound is used to find the size of a large crack under the ground, through which water is flowing. Inside the crack, the ultrasound has a frequency of 28 kHz and a wavelength of 5 cm. A CRO trace shows the two reflected pulses are 130 μs apart.

a)   Calculate the speed of the ultrasound within the crack.

Convert everything to SI units first.

....

....

b)   Calculate the width of the crack, showing your workings.

....

....

....

Top Tips: The really important thing to remember when doing echo questions is that the ultrasound has to travel to the boundary and back, so it's travelled double the distance.

Physics 3(i) — Forces and Waves

Mixed Questions — Physics 3(i)

Q1 Point P marks the pivot point on the wheelbarrow.

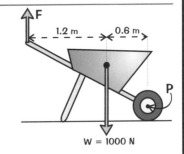

a) Take moments about P to find the **vertical** force, F, that needs to be applied to the handles of the wheelbarrow to just lift it off the ground.

....

....

b) The wheelbarrow tipped over while it was being pushed, fully loaded, across some rocky ground. Explain why this happened using the phrases **resultant moment** and **centre of mass** in your answer.

....

....

Q2 Sarah is experimenting with a CRO and a signal generator connected to a loudspeaker.

She draws a CRO trace for a range of frequencies and amplitudes but gets the labels mixed up.

a) Identify which CRO trace matches each pair of frequency and amplitude values.

Trace	Frequency (Hz)	Amplitude (V)
	100	2
	100	4
	200	2
	200	4
	300	2

b) Would the average human be able to hear all of these sounds? Explain your answer.

....

c) The waveforms above produce pure sounds. On the blank grid on the right, draw a trace that might be produced by a door buzzer.

Q3 This plan view shows two people sitting on a park bench. They can see some statues **reflected** in the window.

a) Use the law of reflection to decide **which of the statues**, A, B, C, and D, persons 1 and 2 can see.

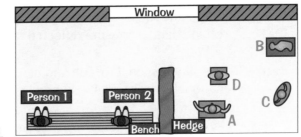

Person 1 ....

Person 2 ....

b) Are the images of the statues **real** or **virtual**? Underline the correct answer.   REAL   VIRTUAL

c) Complete the diagram on the right to show how the image of a statue is formed.

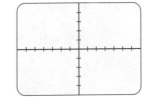

d) If the window were **convex**, the people would be able to see a wider area. Circle the phrases below which would describe the images they would see in a convex mirror.

right-way up   upside-down

bigger than the objects   closer than the focal point

smaller than the objects   further away from the focal point

Mixed Questions — Physics 3(i)

Q4 TV satellite **A** shown below orbits the Earth at a distance of 35 800 km above the surface.

a) What provides the centripetal force that keeps the satellite moving in a circular path?

....

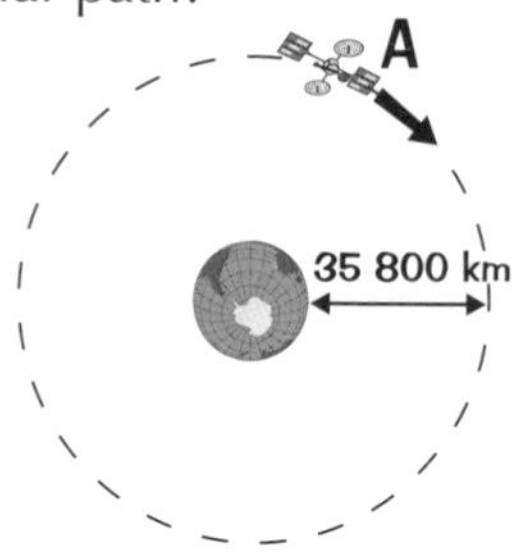

b) What type of satellite is this? Circle the correct answer.

geostationary   **low polar orbit**

c) This type of satellite always travels from west to east,
never from east to west. Explain why this is.

....

d) Indicate whether each of these statements is true or false.

	True	False
i) The satellite is moving at a constant velocity.	☐	☐
ii) The centripetal force acts away from the centre of the circle.	☐	☐

e) **i)** Satellite **B** orbits the Earth at 900 km above the Earth's surface.
Circle the correct words in the short passage below.

> Satellite B experiences a much **stronger** / **weaker** force of attraction than satellite A.
>
> To counteract this, it moves **faster** / **more slowly** than satellite A does.
>
> This means its orbital period is **shorter** / **longer** than that of satellite A.

ii) Suggest a use for satellite **B**. ....

f) Satellite **B** has a cylindrical body coated with shiny metal. Clear reflections appear in it.

i) Explain why you can see clear reflections in shiny surfaces.

....

....

ii) Part of the satellite's body and two incident rays of light are shown
on the right. Draw the **reflected rays** and label the **focal point**.

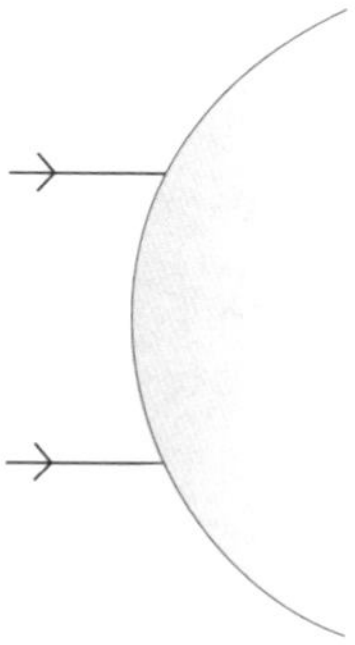

g) Toby is standing on the Earth and can still see the satellite,
even though it has actually dipped below the horizon.

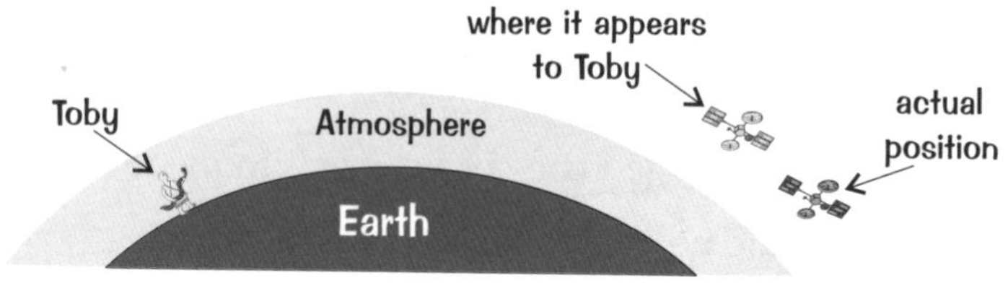

Explain why this is.

....

....

Mixed Questions — Physics 3(i)

Q5   Andrew and Cassie are looking at a shell. They can see it because images form on their **retinas**.

a)   Complete the paths of the light rays on the diagram below.

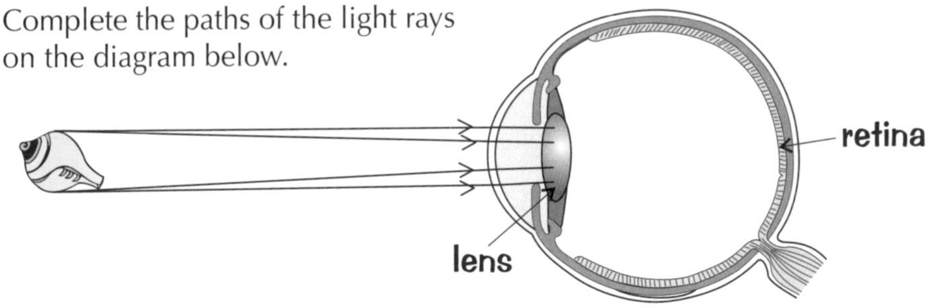

retina

lens

b)   The light entering Cassie's eye is shown in the diagram to the right.
Her lens is working correctly.

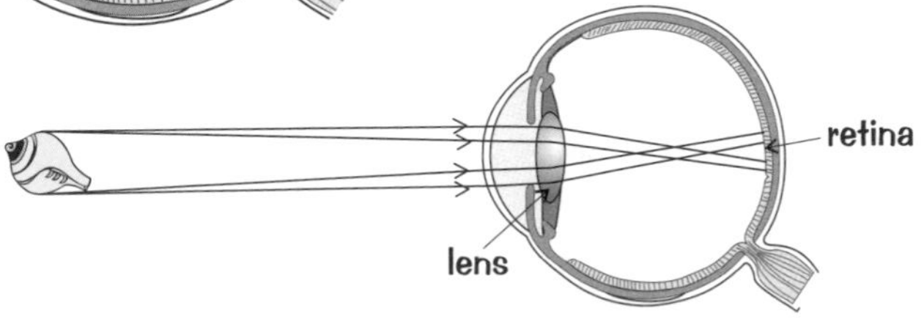

retina

lens

Circle the correct words to complete the sentences below.

Cassie's eyeball is **too** long / short, so images form behind / in front of her retina.

This can be corrected by concave / convex spectacle lenses as these make light rays converge.

c)   Andrew uses a **magnifying glass** to examine the shell, which is 1.8 cm tall. He finds that to magnify the shell, he must hold the lens less than 3 cm from it. When he holds the magnifying glass 2.5 cm away from the shell, the image formed is 4 cm tall.

   i)   What is the focal length of this lens? ....

   ii) What is the magnification of the lens at 2.5 cm? ....

Q6   **Ultrasound imaging** is a valuable technique in many different medical investigations.

a)   A pulse of ultrasound is directed toward an unborn fetus. It **partially reflects** when it reaches the amniotic fluid and again when it reaches the body of the fetus. A CRO trace shows that the time between the reflected pulses is **260 μs**. The frequency of the wave used is 5000 kHz, and its wavelength is 0.003 cm. Calculate how far the fetus is from the outside of the amniotic fluid.

....

....

....

Remember — in 260 μs the pulse travels twice the distance you're calculating.

b)   What substance would you expect an ultrasound wave to travel **fastest** in — **blood**, **muscle** or **air**? Explain your answer.

....

....

c)   A dentist might use ultrasound to clean teeth. Explain how this works.

....

....

Physics 3(ii) — Magnetism and Stars

Magnetic Fields

Q1   Which **one** of the following statements is correct? Tick the box next to the correct statement.

☐   Magnetic fields can only be detected by another magnetic device such as a compass.

☐   Items made from iron, aluminium and steel are all attracted to a magnet.

☐   Magnetic fields can exert a force on a wire carrying a current.

Q2   The diagram below shows a wire carrying a current passing through a piece of flat card.

piece of card

3 V battery

switch

Remember the direction of conventional current flow. Then use the Right-Hand Thumb Rule.

Some iron filings are sprinkled onto the card. When the current is switched on, a pattern develops in the iron filings.

On the diagram, sketch the pattern which the iron filings make, including arrows to show the direction of the magnetic field.

Q3   The diagram below shows a coil of wire (a solenoid) carrying a current.

⊕   ⊖

a)   Draw the shape of the magnetic field around the coil.

b)   Indicate on the diagram where the north and south poles of the electromagnet would be.

c)   What effect would the solenoid have on a piece of soft iron placed near one of its ends?

....

d)   A bar magnet is placed with its north pole nearest to the left-hand end of the coil in the diagram.

i) What force would this magnet experience?

....

ii) Suggest two different ways in which this force could be reversed.

....

....

Magnetic Fields

Q4 The diagram shows how a solenoid can be used as a relay to switch an external circuit on and off.

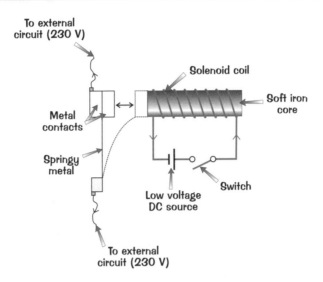

To external
circuit (230 V)

Solenoid coil

Soft iron
core

Metal
contacts

Springy
metal

Low voltage
DC source

Switch

To external
circuit (230 V)

a) Describe what happens when the switch is closed and then opened again.

....

....

....

b) Give two reasons why a **soft iron** core is used in the solenoid.

....

....

c) Explain the effect (if any) of reversing the polarity of the low voltage DC source.

....

....

d) What might you expect to happen if a low voltage AC source were used instead?

....

....

Top Tips: Remember that only **iron**, **steel** (which contains iron), **nickel** and **cobalt** are magnetic. Other metals won't stick to magnets. That's why you often get magnets next to aluminium recycling bins — if a can sticks to the magnet, you know it's **not** aluminium.

The Motor Effect

Q1   Complete the passage below using the words supplied.

| force   angle   stronger   current   magnetic field   permanent magnets |

A wire carrying an electric current has a .... around it.

This can interact with the magnetic fields of other wires or of ....

to produce a .... and sometimes movement. A bigger .... or a

.... magnet will produce a bigger force. The size of the force will also depend

on the .... at which the two magnetic fields meet each other.

Q2   The diagram shows an electrical wire between two magnetic poles.
When the current is switched on, the wire moves at right angles
to the magnetic field.

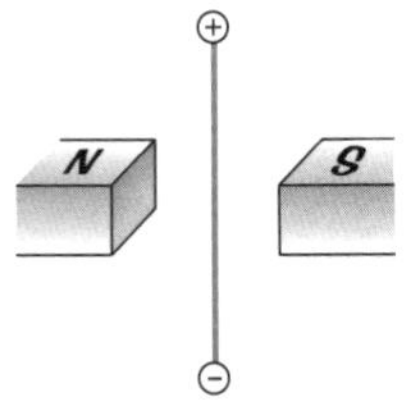

a) Use Fleming's Left-Hand Rule to predict which way the wire will move.

    ....

b) How could the wire be made to move in the opposite direction?

    ....

Q3   Read the three statements below. Tick the box next to each statement that you think is **true**.

☐ A current-carrying wire will not experience a force if it is parallel to the
magnetic field of a permanent magnet.

☐ A current-carrying wire will not experience a force if it is at right-angles
to the magnetic field of a permanent magnet.

☐ A current-carrying wire will not experience a force if it is at an angle of
45° to the magnetic field of a permanent magnet.

Q4   The diagram shows an aerial view of a copper wire carrying a current down into the page.

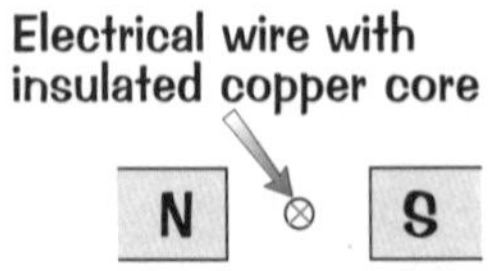

Electrical wire with
insulated copper core

N ⊗ S

State which way the wire will move.

....

The Simple Electric Motor

Q1 Which of the following will **not** make an electric motor spin faster? Tick **one** of the boxes.

☐ Having more turns on the coil.

☐ Using a stronger magnetic field.

☐ Using a soft iron core inside the coil.

☐ Using a bigger current.

☐ Using a commutator.

One of these keeps the motor rotating but does not affect its speed.

Q2 Read the three statements below. Tick the box next to each statement that you think is **true**.

☐ The split-ring commutator makes the motor spin faster.

☐ The split-ring commutator reverses the direction of the current every half turn by swapping the contacts to the DC supply.

☐ The split-ring commutator makes the motor rotate in a different direction.

Q3 Suggest two ways in which the direction of spin of a simple DC motor can be reversed.

....

....

Q4 The electric motor is often used in lifts in tall buildings and mines.
Describe briefly how an electric motor can be used to raise (and lower) a lift cage.

....

....

....

Q5 Use the words supplied to fill in the blanks in the explanation of how a loudspeaker works.

move	amplifier	force	field	sound	magnetic	frequency	current

The loudspeaker relies on the fact that a wire carrying a .... in a

.... can experience a .... A coil is attached to

a cardboard or plastic cone. An AC signal is then sent to the coil from an ....·

This makes the coil .... and causes the cone to vibrate. The cone vibrates at the

same .... as the signal from the amplifier and produces ....·

Electromagnetic Induction

Q1   Look at the apparatus shown in the diagram below.

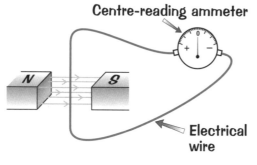

Centre-reading ammeter

Electrical wire

Electromagnetic induction is sometimes called the *generator effect*.

a)   Describe how you could use the apparatus to demonstrate electromagnetic induction.

....

....

b)   What would you see on the ammeter?

....

....

c)   What effect, if any, would the following have:

i) swapping the magnets

....

ii) reversing the connections to the ammeter

....

Q2   A simple generator can be made by rotating a magnet end to end inside a coil of wire.

a)   What happens to the magnetic field when the magnet turns half a turn?

....

b)   What is created in the wire by this rotation?

....

c)   The magnet is constantly turned in the same direction.
Would this generate an AC or DC current in the wire?

....

Electromagnetic Induction

Q3 Moving a magnet inside an electric coil produces a trace on a cathode ray oscilloscope.

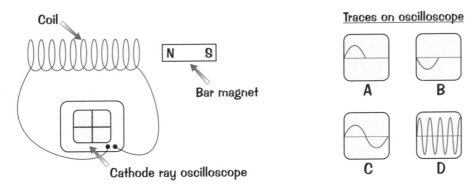

When the magnet was pushed inside the coil, trace A was produced on the screen.

a) Explain how trace B could be produced.

....

b) Explain how trace C could be produced.

....

c) Explain how trace D could be produced.

....

d) Explain how energy is transferred from the moving magnet to the oscilloscope.

....

....

Q4 Look at the simple AC generators sketched below.

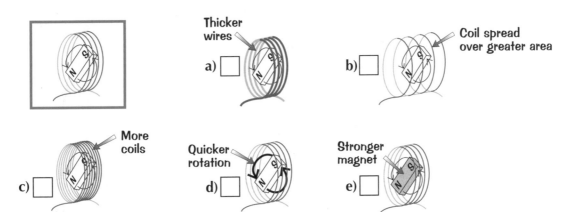

One of the generators labelled **a)-e)** will **not** induce a higher voltage than the generator in the box. Tick the appropriate generator.

Top Tips: Remember that electromagnetic induction is a similar idea to the simple electric motor, but the **other way round**. With the electric motor, a **current** and a **magnetic field** cause **movement**. In electromagnetic induction, **movement** in a **magnetic field** induces a **current**.

Physics 3(ii) — Magnetism and Stars

Generators

Q1   Put each of the features of a DC motor or AC generator into the correct column in the table.

Kinetic energy produced	Kinetic energy consumed	Slip rings	Commutator

DC motor	AC generator

Q2   Explain why the lights on a bicycle with a dynamo dim if the bicycle goes more slowly.

....

....

....

Q3   Complete the energy transfer diagrams below by writing in the correct forms of energy.

.... energy $\longrightarrow$ | Generator | $\longrightarrow$ .... energy

.... energy $\longrightarrow$ | Electric motor | $\longrightarrow$ .... energy

What sort of energy goes in? What sort comes out?

Q4   Which **one** of the statements below about slip rings in an AC generator is **true**? Tick the appropriate box.

☐ The slip rings prevent a current from flowing through the coil of the generator while it is turning.

☐ The slip rings increase the size of the current generated by the coil.

☐ The slip rings reverse the direction of the current supplied to an external circuit every half turn.

Q5   **Steam** can be used to generate electricity in power stations.

a)   What **fuels** are often used to produce steam in power stations?

....

....

b)   The amount of fuel used may affect how fast the coil in the generator spins. How would the display of a connected cathode ray oscilloscope change if the coil of the generator spun faster?

....

....

....

Physics 3(ii) — Magnetism and Stars

Transformers

Q1 The sentences below describe how a **transformer** works but are in the wrong order. Number the boxes 1 to 5 to show the correct order.

☐ The magnetic field produced inside the secondary coil induces an alternating voltage at the ends of the secondary coil.

☐ This produces an alternating magnetic field in the iron core.

☐ An alternating current flows in the primary coil.

☐ If this is applied to an external circuit, an alternating current will flow in that circuit.

☐ A source of alternating voltage is applied to the primary coil.

Q2 Look at the diagram to the right showing two electrical circuits.

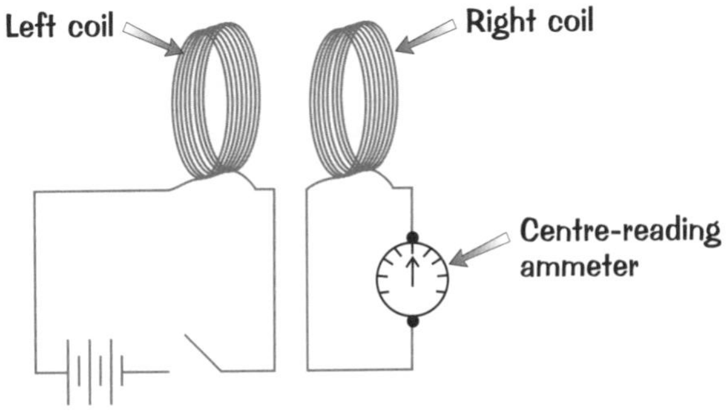

When the switch is closed, a deflection is seen on the ammeter and then the needle returns to zero. When the switch is opened again, a deflection is seen in the opposite direction.

Left coil → Right coil →
Centre-reading ammeter →

a) Explain why this happens.

....

....

b) What could you add to the apparatus to make the needle move further?

....

Q3 Tick the boxes to indicate whether the following statements are **true** or **false**.

	True	False
Step-up transformers have more turns on the primary coil than the secondary coil.	☐	☐
The iron core conducts the current from the primary coil to the secondary coil.	☐	☐
When a transformer is operating it behaves as though a bar magnet was being pushed into and pulled out of the secondary coil.	☐	☐
If you put a DC into the primary coil, a DC will be produced in the secondary coil.	☐	☐

Q4 Many household electrical goods such as computers and radios need a lower voltage than the 230 V mains voltage. What sort of transformer is used to reduce the voltage for these goods?

....

Q5 A transformer is needed to change 200 V to 20 V. If it has 2000 turns on its primary coil, how many turns would the transformer need on its secondary coil?

....

....

Transformers

Q6 A transformer has 100 turns in its primary coil and 4000 turns in its secondary coil. What input voltage would produce an output voltage of 10 000 V?

....

....

Q7 Power stations produce electrical power as an alternating current. Why is this convenient for transmitting power across the **National Grid**?

....

....

Q8 About 8.5% of electricity generated in the UK is lost before it reaches homes and businesses.

a) How is energy "lost" in the National Grid?

....

b) The energy lost in an electrical circuit depends on the current and the resistance of the wires. Use the formulae **P = VI** and **V = IR** to find a formula for power lost in terms of current and resistance.

....

....

c) If a step-up transformer increases the voltage, what does it do to the current?   Hint — use P = V x I.

....

d) Work out the current when 1 MW of power is transmitted at:

i) 250 V ....

ii) 250 000 V ....

e) Use your answers to **a)-d)** to explain fully why and how transformers are used for the National Grid.

....

....

....

....

....

....

Physics 3(ii) — Magnetism and Stars

Stars and Galaxies

Q1 The following sentences explain how new elements were formed after the Big Bang in first generation stars. Rearrange the sentences so that they are in the correct order.

A Once the hydrogen was used up in the stars, helium nuclei began to fuse together to make other, heavier elements.

B Nuclear fusion reactions between hydrogen nuclei in the cores of these stars resulted in the creation of helium nuclei.

C Just seconds after the Big Bang, the Universe contained virtually nothing but hydrogen nuclei.

D Gravitational attraction brought the hydrogen nuclei together to form first generation stars.

Correct order:

.... / .... / .... / ....

Q2 Which one of the following statements is **not true**?
Tick the appropriate box.

☐ Many galaxies contain billions of stars.

☐ The distance between galaxies can be millions of times the distance between stars.

☐ Gravity is the force which keeps stars apart.

☐ Galaxies rotate in space.

☐ Planets are formed from the same clouds of gas and dust as stars.

Q3 When large masses of gas and dust spiral together they form stars.
When smaller masses of gas and dust spiral together they form planets.

Hint — how do stars produce heat?

Explain these two different outcomes.

....

....

Q4 Reactions occur in the cores of stars which produce extremely large amounts of energy.

a) Name the process which releases this energy.

....

b) How is most of the energy released from a star transferred to other parts of the Universe?

....

The Life Cycle of Stars

Q1 A star in its **stable phase** neither expands nor contracts, despite strong forces acting on it. Explain what these forces are, and how the star remains stable.

....

....

Q2 Explain the difference between a **first generation** solar system and a **second generation** solar system.

....

....

....

Q3 The Sun is a main sequence star, but in about 5 billion years time it will become a red giant.

a) What causes a main sequence star to become a red giant?

....

....

b) Why is a red giant red?

....

c) What happens to small stars like our Sun after they become red giants?

....

....

Q4 Some red giants start to undergo more fusion reactions, glow very brightly and then explode.

Give the name of this explosion, and describe what happens after it.

....

....

....

The Life Cycle of Stars

Hint — these bodies have all undergone periods of intense <u>contraction</u>.

Q5   Neutron stars, white dwarfs and black dwarfs are made of matter that is very different from the matter of which planet Earth is made. What is the cause of this difference?

....

....

....

Q6   Below is a diagram showing the life cycles of stars.

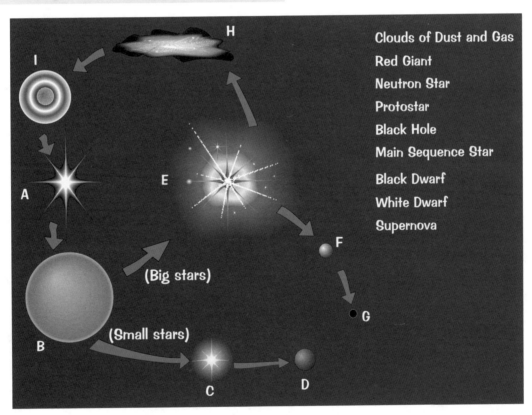

Clouds of Dust and Gas
Red Giant
Neutron Star
Protostar
Black Hole
Main Sequence Star
Black Dwarf
White Dwarf
Supernova

Match the letters to the words on the right of the diagram.

A ....   B ....

C ....   D ....

E ....   F ....

G ....   H ....

I ....

Top Tips: Think of all those billions of stars, and billions of galaxies... incredible. By the way, a billion is taken to mean **10^9** — that's a thousand million, **not** a million million.

Physics 3(ii) — Magnetism and Stars

Mixed Questions — Physics 3(ii)

Q1 The diagram below shows how an **electromagnet** can be used to switch on a car's starter motor.

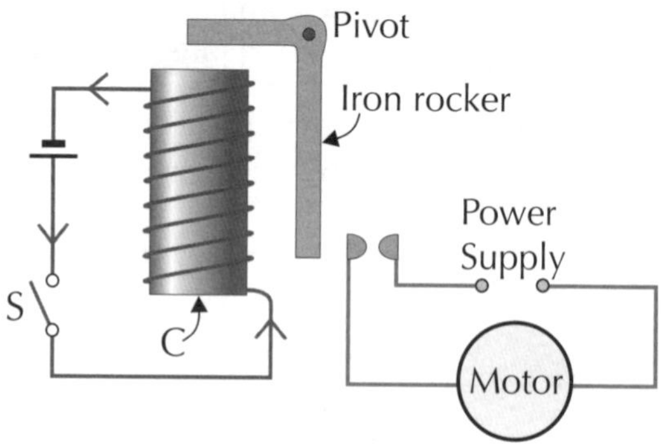

a) What is the function of the iron core, C?

....

....

b) Describe what happens when the switch, S, is closed.

....

....

....

Q2 The diagram below shows a simple **motor**. The coil is rotating as shown.

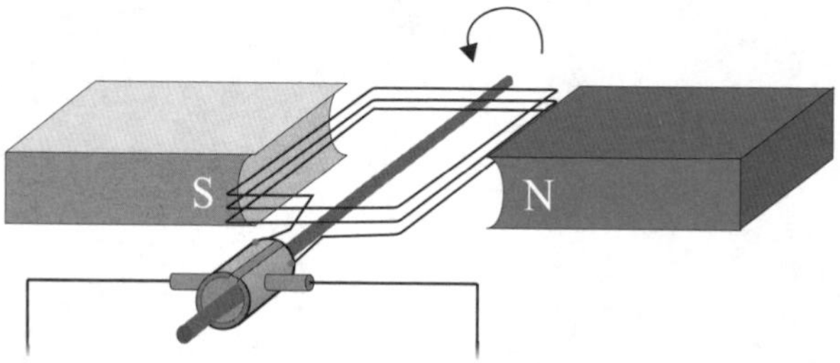

a) On the diagram, draw arrows labelled 'F' to show the direction of the **force** on each arm of the coil.

b) Draw arrows labelled 'I' on each arm of the coil to show the direction the **current** is flowing.

c) Draw a +/– on the leads of the split-ring commutator to show the **polarity** of the power supply.

d) State two ways of increasing the **speed** of this motor.

1. ....

2. ....

Q3 The diagram shows a **bicycle dynamo**.

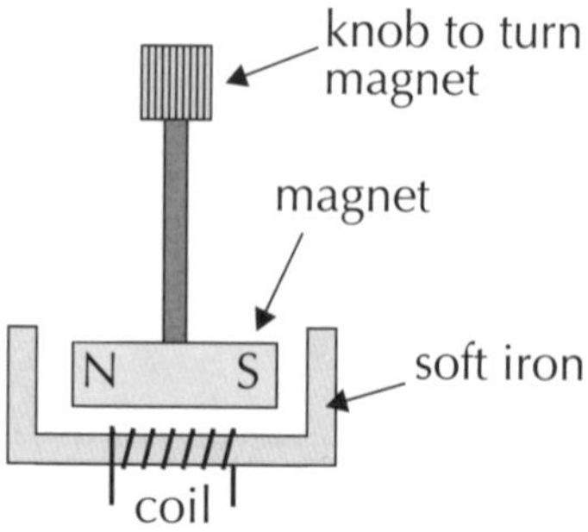

a) What happens in the coil of wire when the knob is rotated **clockwise** at a constant speed? Explain your answer.

....

....

....

b) What would change if the magnet were rotated **anticlockwise** (at the same speed as before)?

....

Mixed Questions — Physics 3(ii)

c) The dynamo is attached to a cathode ray oscilloscope (CRO). When the dynamo is turned, the output is as shown on diagram A.

On Diagram B draw what you would expect to see if the dynamo spins **twice as fast**.

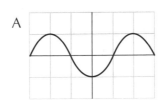 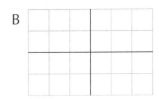

Q4 The diagram shows a **transformer**.

a) What is the output voltage, V?

....

....

b) Transformers are usually wound on a laminated **core**.

i) Name the metal used for the core of the transformer. ....

ii) Why is the core a necessary part of a transformer?

....

....

c) A different transformer is needed to 'step down' a power supply from 33 kV to 230 V. It has 2000 turns on its primary coil. How many turns should it have on its secondary coil?

....

....

d) Explain why transformers only work with **AC** power input.

....

....

....

Q5 The first **stars** were formed by clouds of **hydrogen gas** spiralling in together and getting very **hot**.

a) Why does the gas get hotter as it spirals in?

....

....

b) Explain how very high temperatures lead to the formation of **helium** in a star.

....

....

Mixed Questions — Physics 3(ii)

Q6 A star goes through several stages in its life cycle.

a) **i)** A main sequence star gives off huge amounts of heat and light energy. Explain how such a large amount of energy is produced.

....

ii) Explain why a star is **stable** during its main sequence phase.

....

....

iii) What determines how long the stable period lasts?

....

b) What reactions take place inside a star during its Red Giant stage?

....

....

c) Towards the end of its life a big star explodes in a **supernova**.

i) The explosion leaves behind a very dense core of matter. This core may contract into a **neutron star**. Explain what else could happen to it and why.

....

ii) Describe what happens to the outer dust and debris of the exploding star.

....

Q7 The Earth orbits a **small** main sequence star — the Sun.

a) Explain how planets are formed.

....

....

b) The Earth contains large amounts of heavy elements such as iron. Explain how this provides evidence that the Sun is a **second generation** star.

....

....

....

c) Will the Sun become a **black hole**? Explain your answer.

....

Physics 3(ii) — Magnetism and Stars